Thoughts on The Desperate Church

"Keith has written a thought provoking book that is supremely Biblical and intensely practical. Church members will be encouraged to seek revival and renewal in the church; church leaders will be equipped and inspired to seek God's favor in bringing about revitalization in their churches. As a seminary professor, I plan to use The Desperate Church in my classes. Get this book, read it, and put the principles expounded in it to practice and see what God will do in revitalizing His church!"

Jake Roudkovski
Director, Doctor of Ministry Program
Associate Professor of Evangelism and Pastoral Leadership, New Orleans Baptist Theological Seminary

"Keith Manuel has created a foundational guide to help leaders and congregational members alike align their thinking as they search the Scripture for how to build or revitalize a ministry.
He presents timeless truths of leadership and followership that are essential reading:
-- Be desperate enough for God to humble yourself for His plan and purpose (lead by following)
-- Organize as an organism not as a fixed structure (lead to be adaptive)
-- Look more like Christ (lead to bring others along--patience not pace)
-- Plan and execute with purpose (lead for effective spiritual change, don't just rebrand for effect)

And he offers even more, emphasizing everything within the spheres of prayer and the Word.

It is the worth the read and re-read for anyone in any congregation--of any size, setting, style or stage of life-- seeking to be purposeful for the Kingdom in revitalizing or building a ministry.

Will Hall, Ph.D.
Editor, The Baptist Message
Former Vice President of News Services with the Southern Baptist Convention Executive Board and Crusade Director for Go Tell Ministries

"Packed with wisdom and specific help church leaders can put into practice immediately, if they are serious about their congregation's health and motivated to increase its effectiveness. Brilliant thinking and writing... a fresh look at timeless truths... a much-needed resource. Most important factor that makes this book stand-out: The Desperate Church rings true with authority and authenticity. This author has "been there" -- and succeeded."

Carolyn Curtis
Author or collaborator of seven books. Most recently, *Women and C.S. Lewis*. She is published in *On Mission, Facts & Trends, Sports Illustrated,* and *The Saturday Evening Post* to name a few.

The current situation in Southern Baptist Churches is alarming. Dr. Keith Manuel has worked with churches helping them revitalize their ministries. He has basically led them to address immediate current needs and access their ministries for long term growth. Dr. Manuel has written a marvelous book for the pastor or layman who wishes to help their church go from decline to growth. Using the acronym "BUILD" as the foundation for his work, Dr. Manuel challenges the reader to examine certain characteristics of church revitalization.

Even though Dr. Manuel states that the book is not a "how to book on church revitalization," he does in fact, write with the purpose of renewal in mind. Manuel address the organization structure, the role of leadership within the process, and finally the attitude of the church i.e. is the church humble enough to address their situation.

This is a must read for the pastor, layman and congregation. In my opinion, this work would make a great Wednesday Night Study or a special committee study.

Marvin Jones
Chair, Division of Christian Studies
Assistant Professor of Christian Studies,
Lousiana College.

The Desperate Church would make an excellent small group or Wednesday study for a congregation, as well as for a group of pastors, and of course for an individual. There are thought and discussion provoking study questions at the end of each chapter, followed by a soul searing prayer.

It opens with the need of a person or people in a church to be absolutely desperate for God to be evident in their life or lives. Without a sense of desperation, nothing will change.

This well written book -- it flows smoothly at every moment -- shoots straight. Author Keith Manuel doesn't soft peddle his words. It is as if he is saying, "If you are serious, here is what you can do. If you are not serious, don't even bother because

God won't be in your efforts." Or, to say it another way, " God works when you do things His way."

While the author includes some illustrations and good ideas, mainly he provides and explains principles -- of leadership, of pastoral care, of church discipline, and of course of evangelism. Reading The Desperate Church showed me how desperate I am for a revival in my relationship with God and with my church. The people in my church need to read it so we are all on the same page as we encourage each other to be more Christlike as we live out our faith in our daily lives.

The Desperate Church is one of those books you are going to want to buy 20 or 30 copies of, so you have plenty to share.

Karen Willoughby
Retired Managing Editor, The Baptist Message
Recepient of "Award of Excellence for Denominational Leadership in Journalism"

Manuel's book pushes the envelope in church leadership. From the start there is a great desire to get back to God and the basics. This book is challenging, not just to the layman or the staff, but to the pastor as well. There is a call for God's leaders to do whatever it takes, within the realm of scripture, to reach across the pew in love and reach out in the community for the sake of others. I highly recommend this book to pastors, staff, laymen, and anyone willing to be awakened to the power of God in their life, church, and community! Great opportunity for a pastor and staff related study!

Joshua Adams
Pastor, Pisgah Baptist Church

The Desperate Church

Asking God For A Fresh Start Through Prayer and Planning

Keith Manuel

Hidden Pearl Publishing
Pineville, LA

For my family whom I love. Wendy, Keith, Jr., Jeremy, and Hannah, you are blessings to me.

Finally, thanks to the congregations who allow me to experiment with ideas both big and small. You bring glory to our Lord.

The Desperate Church Contents

CHAPTER ONE

BECOMING A DESPERATE CHURCH

Asking the Holy Spirt for Spiritual Brokenness

There comes a moment in the life of a church when it becomes defeated or desperate enough to change. Statistics reveal that 70-90 percent of churches are in decline or have plateaued. It doesn't mean these churches are not functioning. They are like an older automobile, not hitting on all cylinders. Some have more damage than others do, but all are in danger of becoming irrelevant.

Not all churches are in terrible shape. Some need minor tweaking. Even a healthy church needs to evaluate what they are doing and why they are doing it. The way to remain healthy is to examine the work and make sure the foundation remains solid. The leaders of a healthy church need to make sure they are doing everything possible to ensure the body does not become complacent and apathetic. Many unhealthy churches were at one time healthy.

THE DESPERATE CHURCH

What will it take in order to awaken a church? What will have to occur in the church to make the radical shift to come alive? Church leaders and consultants can analyze where a church is strong or weak. That may be a start. However, desperation for God is a collective response of godly people. Either it is there or it is not. Desperation enables a broken body of believers to embrace the hard work of spiritual renewal. Then God empowers you to carry out the mental, physical and spiritual tasks of revitalization.

I've had the privilege to lead multiple churches through a process of resetting as pastor or interim pastor. Several were in small towns. One was in a major urban center and two were in rural communities. One church was in an extremely rural setting. The principles have been the same for the church of 40 members and the church with more than 1,200 members. Some have become more vibrant than others have, but all turned a corner in their focus. I've also had the opportunity to serve as a consultant for several hundred churches trying to work through a similar process. It is hard work. It is tedious work. To make this radical shift, it takes a spiritual, emotional, and physical overhaul that is intentional. The church and those leading the change must remain focused on their purpose. They must become so desperate for God that they begin to make changes no one ever imagined they could make. Some churches will become desperate temporarily, some long term. However, I want to give you a personal word out of my experience. It is possible for your church to be renewed. To what degree that happens depends on you, as the body of Christ, surrendering to Jesus.

To lead a church through a process of faithful surrendering requires strategic planning. As you begin this journey and you start formulating ideas of what the church needs to accomplish, most people will realize the magnitude of the need and wonder where to start. There are two options for leaders. The first is to find where the energy is within the church family and start there. A second option is to decide where the leaders can affect change by themselves and start a wave of momentum.

Surfing provides a good analogy for this decision. A surfer studies the ocean to observe when a wave that suits his ability is approaching. Next, when he decides to catch a wave, he begins to paddle his board to get forward momentum until the wave carries him along. If he paddles too little, the wave passes him by. If he paddles too soon, he gets himself out of position to get the most out of the wave. Sometimes, he chooses the wrong wave and bails out. When he times it right, there is an exhilarating ride. Whichever wave the surfer chooses will only last a short time and requires him to paddle back out and catch another wave. A surfer doesn't create a wave, but he does choose when and where to surf. Good decisions at this point will determine the outcome.

The Place to Start

You may be thinking that sounds fine, but where do I start? Start by looking back and see if there is a wave already coming in your direction. Maybe the church has energy for some element of need that will lead toward a new zeal for service. If there is no wave of momentum, choose the area you can affect the most that will cause the least amount of discord and work on that area. Great leaders learn to give the church victories early and often. This builds trust when you begin to deal with the harder areas of revitalization. You can't do everything at once and you don't want to build momentum for change, then lose it. Momentum is hard to build in a church. However, when the momentum shifts, learn to use that as a time to reevaluate, renew your own energy and then select new areas on which to work as the next wave of momentum builds.

A key to revitalization is to understand it's a marathon, not a footrace. It doesn't happen overnight. There will be challenges along the way. Some of the work will be exhilarating and some of it will be devastating. The reality is both of these emotional reactions may occur on the same day or even during the same hour. That's why there is a high degree of burnout among pastors and church members who lead this charge. Many will want to quit. Some do. For some, it is easier to die than to do the work God uses to bring life back to the declining or dying church.

Currently, there is a major move toward church planting. The old saying is, "It's easier to give birth than to resurrect the dead." Many young pastors would rather start something new than to deal with the entrenched leadership and traditions of a dying or plateaued church. Honestly, there is an excitement to the concept of starting something from scratch. Even in this scenario, a person wanting to plant a church needs to understand exciting doesn't equate to easy. Church planting is hard work and has many challenges. However, when looking at plateaued churches, there are good churches that need help, who want help, and will be glad to turn over the reigns to a pastor who will love them and lead them. From a practical standpoint, we have invested millions of dollars into people and properties. It would be poor stewardship to abandon the people and sell the properties for pennies on the dollar unless there is no opportunity to reach people in that location.

After Hurricane Katrina, experts told pastors in the New Orleans area and the Mississippi Gulf Coast that historically there is an 80 percent turnover in church staff following a major crisis. That statistic was accurate. Some turnover came from burnout and some came from new opportunities as churches in other areas observed leadership qualities in these hardworking men and women. Another statistic was 80 percent of pastors leave after leading a church through a major building campaign. What does this mean? Change brings change. Not always. But, many times.

Mark Twain said, "No one likes change but a wet baby." Change is difficult. However, for a healthy organization, change is necessary. For a struggling, dying church, change must occur. It is very accurate to say not everyone will be on board with change. In fact, some who say they are 100 percent supportive of change will change. Suddenly, because of pressure from friends, family, or strangers they will reverse their position. An old saying is, "We will not be different until the pain of staying the same becomes greater than the pain of change." Here is the real question, "Do you want the church you attend to die?"

THE DESPERATE CHURCH

There are some things you can examine to determine if the church you attend or lead is about to die. Look at your track record of evangelism. Are people being saved and connecting with your church? A ten-year study is very enlightening as to whether a church is on a downward swing. Look at the average age of your membership. A healthy church is well balanced with children, youth, young adults, median adults and senior adults. A dying church is often filled with a large majority of senior adults with little to no children or youth. Look at your small group Bible study numbers. Are you flat-lined or declining in attendance? Look at the number of new members versus members lost to death or relocation. When was the last time you started a new class because of growth?

Understanding these challenges, a church must set its course. It must decide to die or become desperate for change. As a matter of fact, making no decision is a decision to die. A dying church will attempt to fix a few things, but it will become easily frustrated without quick results and go back to the norm. A desperate church will do many things and seek to find what works. A dying church struggles against the current. A desperate church catches a wave, rides it and paddles out to catch another. A dying church will not change. They will only shift from side to side, always coming back to dead center, moving toward a slow death. A desperate church will shift, but move closer to God and closer to life. A dying church is in love with the organization and looks to the past. A desperate church is in love with Jesus and looks to the future. A dying church focuses internally. A desperate church fixes the internal and focuses on the external. A dying church is controlled by a small group of people. A desperate church gives control to the Spirit of God to use whomever He will. A dying church tries to hang on to a monument. A desperate church is seeking to resurrect a ministry.

Dying vs. Desperate

In a dying church apathy reigns supreme. Many will say, "If the lost would only come, we have teachers, classes, and special events ready for them." This may burst your bubble, but it is a reality. Lost people driving by your church could not care less what you are doing on the inside of your church. They don't care that you have crayons and carpet in your children's rooms. They don't care that you have nice, air conditioned buildings and a recently renovated worship space. They don't care that you are friendly to one another. They don't care that you have covered dish dinners. They don't care that you have well-trained teachers and adequate parking for growth. Don't get me wrong. Most of them aren't opposed to your church being there. Many of them like the fact that there are churches in their community. They just don't think about you or really care what you are doing on the inside of the church. They are busy trying to raise kids, get the grass cut, go on vacation, fix the car, enjoy a hobby or simply relax between workdays. They are too busy to think about you. They don't have time for you. That is why a growing church goes to them and takes the information to them. A healthy church shows the lost world the value Jesus brings to their lives.

THE DESPERATE CHURCH

A dying church is busy fussing and fighting over every area of ministry. Instead of a budget that guides spending, every single purchase or expenditure must go through a committee and a business meeting that is a knock-down-drag-out. If you don't understand it, let me be the first to tell you, the lost are not going to be a part of a fighting church. Furthermore, young adults are not going to participate in a church where every time they have an idea of how to serve the Lord, they have to go through a bureaucratic nightmare to get started. There is enough bureaucracy and fighting in the workplace that the majority of people will look at a church that stifles the work of the Lord or fights over the work of the Lord and say, "I will not subject my family or myself to this environment." Many healthy churches grow simply because they don't fight and every other church around them is in constant turmoil.

One of the quickest ways to run off your young adults is to run off or fire church staff and/or the pastor. Many churches, once they start firing staff rarely stop. It becomes easier to do every time they do it. It's as if they are a bunch of sharks smelling blood in the water. On many occasions, it boils down to one or two people making the decision its time for the pastor to go. This small group usually makes the decision over personality conflicts or personal preferences, not biblical grounds. These few make enough noise until they get a committee or some form of leadership to offer a severance package that is usually hush money so the pastor doesn't let the church know what really happened or why and how he decided to resign. The group threatens the pastor with: "If you aren't quiet about what we've told you, the severance is gone." These groups want the pastor or staff member to have great accountability. However, these people don't want anyone to know the details of their deceit. The amazing thing is, the next pastor who comes along can't do anything right either.

A church that continually fights and fires staff needs to look in the mirror and realize the problem is themselves. Until the church corrals the bullies and unprincipled people who are controlling the church, it will continue to decline. Many times, because a church refuses to exercise biblical discipline, a few church members will sway a vote of the church or even a call to ministers simply on a whim. The church suffers because of a lack of accountability among members for their actions. Some people feel that because they are a member, they can say or do whatever they want. Either troublemakers are dealt with in a restorative, godly manner, or the church will continue to move toward ineffectiveness or even death. The worship center will become a crypt with pews where the few who remain only look back with sunken eyes to the glory days and complain about the unfaithful who abandoned their church. They stand around staring at a pale church on life support, contemplating when they should pull the plug.

There are times when the need exists for a leadership change and the church needs to make hard decisions. However, it should be a godly process and a restorative process. If a pastor is lacking a certain skill that more than a few thinks he needs, get him help and love him through it, just as you would want the church to do for you. If the leadership decides it would be best for the pastor to move to another field of service, work with him so that it is a good transition for all. If there is gross neglect or immorality, most churches have a clearly defined process for that journey too.

Revitalization can come even to a notorious church that likes to fight. However, it will take a concerted effort on the part of such a church to repent and begin the restorative work to fix the internal conflict. The next step is to move to an external focus on reaching the world for Christ.

When Jesus BUILDs the Church

Since Jesus said, "I will build my church" (Matt. 16:18b), we can ask Him to direct the work of revitalization. Churches that are ready for this process will exhibit certain characteristics seen in the word *BUILD*.

> **Brokenness:** Until a church assumes a position of humility, desperation, and brokenness, restoration cannot occur. It must be Jesus' church, not ours.

> **Unity:** A church must unify in the purpose and calling of Christ. The people must serve together.

> **Innovation:** Building implies change. We must change our methods, while never changing our message.

> **Love:** If we love God and then love our neighbors, we will be a church that goes to and attracts hurting people.

BECOMING DESPERATE

Dedication: It's not going to be easy. Working with Jesus as He builds is hard, sometimes grueling work. However, it is always worth it.

This book is not a how-to book on church revitalization. It does examine three areas that are vital to revitalization. These three are interspersed throughout the chapters, in no particular order. First, we will ask questions about the organizational aspects of the church. Without an effective organization, the church is set on a course of chaos. Many churches have too much organization and work themselves to death to maintain the organization. An organization should look like an organism not a monument. It should grow, change, and take the shape of the needs of the work of the Lord. You will remove nothing that is biblically mandated. However, anything that is an organizational tradition should be analyzed and open to change.

If the people you are trying to reach wanted what you are currently offering, they would already be at your church. This is one of those in-your-face kinds of statements. You need to hear it clearly. That doesn't mean you throw out everything. It does mean you examine everything, especially whether your ministry focus is inward, focused on taking care of the flock, or outward, looking for the lost sheep. You need both, but a dying church always focuses on itself, trying to make sure the organization survives. It's all about maintaining the monument. The thought is, "I can't imagine my church not existing." Instead, the thought ought to be, "I can't imagine my neighbor going to hell." What a dying church needs is people. New people.

People committed to Jesus. People committed to the task of evangelism and discipleship. Personally and collectively.

Second, we will look at the spiritual elements of revitalization. Some churches need to change internally. They are not walking with the Lord, much less allowing the Spirit of the Lord to lead. When you examine them, they are not acting or functioning as a biblical community. You need to ask questions about how to lead a church to grow beyond their current state. A healthy church looks more like Christ, not less.

Finally, we will examine leadership characteristics and opportunities for a church wanting to revitalize. Not every pastor received training to lead through revitalization. Not everyone has the stomach for it. It is definitely not for a person who is easily dissuaded or discouraged. You must enter revitalization with the confidence of Christ and a solid view of yourself. You must know your strengths and weaknesses. You must be willing to listen to godly wisdom, especially when the advice is opposed to your plan. As a leader, you must be willing to change, just as you are going to ask the church to be willing to make changes.

There is not a "one-size fits all" model that can fix plateaued or dying churches. Out of much study, I can assure you there are no "silver bullets" that anyone can show you to help a church recover. However, there are some questions pastors, church leaders, and church members can ask our Lord to determine if they are willing to follow the leadership of the Holy Spirit.

Not all the questions that need to be asked are in this book, but it is a start. Many will start with the wrong question of, "Can God revitalize this church?" It is never about what God can do. God can do it. The real question is, "Will this group of people do the work necessary for the church to be revitalized?" More indepth is, "Will this group of people allow God to change them to be used in revitalization?"

As a leader, you must ask yourself these two questions. Am I willing to do the work necessary and will I allow God to change me? You may have to start with a personal retreat. Get away to search the will of God and examine your own heart. Then you can move to leading others through a staff/leader retreat or a weekly time with leaders to pose these questions to God. Make sure you give others the time necessary to catch the same vision. You probably didn't arrive at your decision overnight. Don't expect others to embrace revitalization without time to fast, pray and search God's Word.

When you do ask God about revitalization, listen for His answers. Listen to His Spirit speaking through His Word. I am praying for you in this journey. Others are praying for you. Your community needs you to be healthy and growing. The community of faith needs you to be alive and shine the light of Christ in your world. Grow desperate and allow Christ to build His church. Grow bold and move from the comfort of the plateau. It will take prayer. It will take planning. It will take you, as a body, becoming desperate for God.

DISCUSSION QUESTIONS

1. Do we expect revitalization to come quickly to our church? Why or why not?

2. How can we encourage our pastor and leaders during our study? During an effort for revitalization?

3. Are we more inwardly focused or outwardly focused as a church?

4. Can and will our current church members do the work necessary to see our church revitalized?

PRAYER

Lord,
Break my heart to be moldable by you. As you change me, you will change our church. Help me to see what you see, do what you do, and live how you lived. Fix my brokenness and strengthen my weaknesses for your glory and for your name.
In Jesus' Name.
Amen.

CHAPTER TWO

ARE WE DESPERATE FOR GOD

Holy Spirit, Are We Seeking You for Restoration?

Throughout this book, you will ask the Holy Spirit to lead you to answers. Jesus said the Holy Spirit would teach us all things and He would remind us of the things Christ taught (John 14:26). The first questions you will ask the Holy Spirit is, "Are we desperate enough to seek only You to bring restoration to this congregation? Are we desperate enough to allow You to move us in any way you would like to move us?"

It is obvious that if we ask questions that are at the heart of God, He will answer clearly. The Bible says, Now this is the confidence we have before Him: Whenever we ask anything according to His will, He hears us. And if we know that He hears whatever we ask, we know that we have what we have asked Him for (1 John 5:14-15, HCSB). The warning is to make sure what you are hearing agrees with the Word of God. The Bible is our final authority. What we hear, if it is from God, will never conflict with the Bible.

God's Power

Look at this statement again; "Until a church gets to the place that the pain of change outweighs the pain of staying the same, little will happen." Many churches are trapped in the worship of tradition instead of the Savior. Until the only things that are sacred are the truths in the Word of God, the church hasn't come to a place of desperation.

Make no mistake; not everything a dying church is doing needs to be discarded. This is not a throwing out of the proverbial baby with the bath water. However, you should give an honest review to everything your congregation does to see if it is necessary and if it moves the church toward life.

Some churches will need to completely start over with new committees and leaders. Others will need to tweak what they are doing already by getting rid of organizations that hold them back or are no longer working.

Still, other churches are so busy doing church, they miss the reason they exist. Families are at the church so much that they never have any time to be a family. Their church members are tired and worn out. Many churches in this condition even pressure their members with a passive aggressiveness by insinuating the members are less spiritual if they don't give up everything else to be at church every night of the week. Some churches are doing so many things that they are doing none well. Most things they do are mediocre. Some ministries are so flighty that they jump on every bandwagon that comes along. They change ideas midstream, trying their best to stay current or to find the magic formula that will transform their downward spiral, without ever completing the original task. Busyness does not connote godliness or health. The flighty church or minister will constantly frustrate the staff and/or the church. It is better to do a few things well, than to do many things poorly.

The opposite of this is true too. A church that never attempts great things for God can expect to have very little that succeeds for God. The goal should be to fail at several things in order to find the few things that work well. Not everything you do needs to be a success. However, everything you do should lead to your next opportunity for success. Failing churches say, "We've already tried that." Successful churches say, "It is an appropriate time to try this again."

The problem for some dying churches is they are functioning as they always have, but they are doing it without the Spirit of the Lord. Jesus addressed the church at Ephesus in Revelation 2. He told them He knew all that they were doing and that they were working exceedingly hard. The church had overcome obstacles from the external pressures of an ungodly world to internal pressures of false teachers. However, here was their problem. They left their first love. They were good at the second great commandment of loving their neighbors as they love themselves. But, they were not good at the first commandment — the Great Commandment — love the Lord your God with all your heart, soul, and strength. Someone said, "What would a church look like the Sunday after the Spirit of the Lord left the building?" The answer is – the exact same as the Sunday before. Nothing would change. The church would probably never notice. A church without the Spirit of the Lord is busy doing good things. It is busy doing God-like things. However, it is not doing them in the power and the presence of the Lord.

God's Charge

Desperation leads a church to humble itself before the Lord, asking Him to change them. Humility, prayer and seeking the face of God leads to the turning from wickedness in the often-quoted renewal passage of 2 Chronicles 7:14.

Humility is important to revitalization because we understand it is beyond our power to bring renewal. We need God. We need God to enable us to change for His glory.

The Lord demands humility. On the journey to the Promised Land, He reminded the Hebrew children that He was their provider. The Lord said to remember He brought them out of Egypt. He provided manna to eat in the desert and water to drink. He protected them from their enemies. He provided even for the swelling of their feet. So, when entering into the Promised Land, they must be careful to remember — it is the Lord who provides everything, even the power to gain wealth. Nothing is of our own making. The Lord Himself provides for His children (Deuteronomy 8).

It is very easy to make the mistake that it is within our power to change a dying church. We don't make the change.

We become an agent of change that the Lord uses. Many times, it is the least likely candidate whom the Lord uses to bring about renewal.

However, it is within our power to pray. Prayer is not a way to inform God of our desires and needs. Prayer is used by God to inform us of our need for Him. We don't have the answers, the power, or the ability to change the world for His glory. However, He does. That is why we need prayer — to recognize our need and to realize His sufficiency.

When the church is in peril, we need to come before His throne, boldly, on behalf of the body of Christ. We need to admit to Him our desperation and our utter inability to make the changes without His leadership and guidance. As we pray, putting our need before a righteous God, His Holy Spirit begins to work in our lives through His peace and presence. We begin to get a sense of comfort and conviction.

When we recognize the sufficiency of Christ and the power of the Holy Spirit dwelling in us, we will want to seek His face. The God who knows all is willing to communicate with us. To share his knowledge with us. To share his heart with us. He loves us enough to let us draw near to Him. We may not be able to recline upon the physical presence of the Lord as John did, but we can lean on His understanding, instead of our own. In all of our ways, we can acknowledge Him. In the moments when we do this, He will direct our paths (Proverbs 3:5-6). Trust Him. Seek Him. Find His Heart.

The final element of the renewal directive of Chronicles is to turn from our wicked ways. Sometimes the change needs to come from the lives of the leaders. Is personal sin blocking the flow of the Spirit's blessings in your life and in the lives of the people you lead? Is there corporate sin in the life of the church that is blocking the blessings of the Spirit of the Lord? Is that sin threatening the unity of the body, the health of the body, or the direction of the body? Is there a committee or team that is not seeking the Lord's face but is self-serving and bringing harm to the faithful? Have you been busy taking care of the organization and working hard in the community, but have left your first love? You love your neighbor as yourself, but you don't love the Lord Your God with all your heart, soul, and strength. Repent. Turn from sin and self. Turn toward Jesus, the Savior. It's His church. Become desperate for Him and He will take care of His church.

God's Church

God is looking for churches that will let Him lead. Actually, Psalm 127 tells us that unless the Lord builds the house, the laborers work in vain. We are not to be church architects. We are to be the labor force under the direction of the One who designs the church. Our pastors are to lead us to follow the Lord's blueprint, so our Foundation is sure. One of the great hymns of faith says, "On Christ the Solid Rock I stand. All other ground is sinking sand."

When the church becomes our church and not the Lord's church there is a huge problem. At that very moment, we might as well shut the doors, change the sign and label it as our new clubhouse, fraternity, sorority, social club, or whatever term we choose to use. What it is not, at that point, is a church. The church is the Lord's. He is to direct the work. We are to accomplish the task.

God calls church members to collectively be followers who take up their crosses daily and follow Him. We are to die to self and sin. We are to be alive for Jesus. When we exemplify Christ, we show the world a picture of a Servant willing to lay down His life for his sheep.

Some church members act like consumers instead of worshipers. By their actions and attitudes they say, "I came here for you to die for me. You serve me." Instead, they should have the attitude of Jesus, "The Son of Man did not come to be served but to serve, and to give his life as a ransom for many" (Mark 20:28).

While church discipline is a tricky subject, there has become a feeling that anything goes in the body of Christ. A false belief that if someone points out the sin in the church or in a church member's life is judging that one and should look at their own lives and not say anything about the sin. That is partly true. Jesus, in Matthew 7, presents the teaching not to judge, then gives the thought of removing the log out of one's own eye first. However, listen to the rest of His statement, "then you will see clearly to take the speck out of your brother's eye." Jesus calls believers to be a redemptive people, not a passive people. The body of Christ cannot allow just anything to continue within its ranks. Fallen people, of all people, should judge each other with a righteous judgment in order to be a shining light to the world. Jesus' teaching is a clear teaching about not having a constant critical spirit. It is a warning that we should be looking deeply in our hearts to correct our own discretions.

However, He also calls us to correct and reprove one another with love.

One of the rules of interpreting Scripture is when a passage is difficult to interpret its full meaning then you allow the rest of Scripture to shed light on the passage in order to understand the meaning. In fact, later in Matthew 18, Jesus gives us a direct teaching of how to deal with a personal wrong in the body of Christ. If someone sins against a fellow believer, the offended party is to confront that individual and tell the offender of the hurt. If the offender repents, then the two walk in harmony again. If the offender refuses, then the offended is to bring two or three believers to try to correct the offense. If it can't be worked out on this occasion, then a larger group, the church, is to help redeem the situation. At that point, if the one is still unrepentant, the church is to treat that person as someone outside the church. In the New Testament, that does not mean never having anything to do with that one. It means to reach out to that one, even though the church is to cut off him or her from the daily life of the church until repentance occurs.

Look at the other examples of this in Scripture. In 2 Thessalonians, Paul admonishes his readers if one does not follow his teaching from the Lord in this letter, to have no company with this one, but not to treat this offender as an enemy. However, the church is to admonish him or her as a fellow believer. In 2 Corinthians 2, Paul discusses one who has caused pain to the church at Corinth. After a time of discipline, Paul encourages the church to go to that one to forgive and to give comfort, so that person will not be excessively sorrowful. He exhorts them to show that one love. It is clear in Scripture that the body of Christ is to hold individuals accountable for their actions that harm the church, but that accountability should lead the individual to restoration. The actions of the church should be tempered with love for Christ and love for all. Remember, God demonstrated his love for us in that while we were still sinners, Christ died for us (Romans 5:8).

Back to the context of Jesus' words in Matthew 18, the church is to act with the authority of the Lord, binding forgiveness and discipline, not arbitrarily but with the Lord in their midst. The church often takes the verses in 19-20 out of context. Here the two who agree on anything (pragma in Greek), are agreeing about a judicial matter, as the word pragma is most frequently used. But as a third party is introduced, the Lord himself also sees and agrees that the situation of the offense should be handled appropriately. His authority is given for the rectifying of the situation.

Two more overarching ideas must guide our actions in this scenario of discipline. First, while Jesus gives the steps in sequential order, the idea is to handle the offense in the least public way before the offense has to be handled in the most public manner. This is not to be a cover-up; it is to be a covering. It is to provide the offender every opportunity to find forgiveness, love and restoration through the covering of the blood of the Savior in the least public way possible. The next conversation between Peter and Jesus (18:21-35) provides the second overarching idea to discipline. How often is the church or individuals to forgive the repentant believer? Jesus makes it clear, as often as true repentance occurs. Believers are to be merciful and loving toward repentant people, no matter how grievous the offense, as often as Jesus has forgiven you. If you treat one of the Lord's children horribly, Jesus himself will hold you to account. Believers should handle these hard truths with care and with great discretion. Discipline and accountability show us that we can't act without affecting others. It also shows our need for guidance from the Lord.

God's Vision

God is looking for people who are utterly dependent on Him. God is looking for churches that will be utterly dependent on Him. The old saying is, "Work like it completely depends on you. Pray like it completely depends on God." Ask God to give you the vision He wants the church to embrace. Ask God to give you the attitude He wants in a church.

Many studies of revitalization will lead to someone quoting, "Where there is no vision, the people perish" (Proverbs 29:18). However, the inverse is just as true, "Without the people, the vision perishes." We need both leaders and followers, with all being submissive to the will of God. A leader who gains a vision of the work God calls the church to undertake must enlist the people to be God's willing workers. A leader helps the people catch the vision.

Becoming desperate doesn't mean becoming incapacitated. However, it does mean understanding God's strength is your support. God's purpose becomes your purpose. God's will becomes your will. You hate the things God hates. You love the things God loves. You serve the way God served. You seek what God calls you to seek. You stop what God calls you to stop. You go where God tells you to go. You do what God commands you to do. You become desperate to be where God wants you to be. No one else is above God. No one else is sufficient. Nothing else is a priority.

Ike Reighard, a pastor and motivational speaker who has led churches in revitalization, said, "Jesus didn't say, 'It is finished,' so you can say, 'I quit!'" It is about giving every thing up to God, in order to give your all for God.

The beauty of the poetry in the Psalm 63:1 is so clear in the King James Version and conveys the longing of one who is desperate for God. "O God, thou art my God; early will I seek thee: my soul thirsteth for thee, my flesh longeth for thee in a dry and thirsty land, where no water is." As a church, we should come thirsty, begging God to give us a drink of the cool water of life. One who is desperate begs for a great God to restore life in His church. Ask again, "Holy Spirit, are we truly desperate for You to do a work of restoration in this church body?"

DISCUSSION QUESTIONS

1. Am I desperate enough to allow the Holy Spirit to change me and then to change our church as a whole?

2. What are traditional programs and what are biblically mandated programs of our church? Make a list of everything you do as a church and mark it as traditional or biblical.

3. Spend a moment in silent contemplation and prayer. Ask God to show you any unconfessed sin in your life or any attitudes that need to be changed in order for God to move in your life and the life of the church.

4. Pray for your pastor and leaders of the church to be open to what God would have you to do as a group of people seeking revitalization for your congregation.

PRAYER

Lord,
You are the healer and the unifier of people. Make our hearts unite around what matters most to you. May we love with unconditional love. May we act with boldness and conviction. In Jesus' Name.
Amen.

CHAPTER THREE

LEADING WITH POWER

Holy Spirit, Do I Need a Renewed Passion to Lead?

The role of the pastor is key to a successful revitalization. This should come as no surprise because without a bold leader very few organizations change. Some churches go through a period of change and the church receives a new pastor. The new pastor brings excitement and fervor to the congregation along with fresh ideas to shepherd God's sheep and reach the community. Other churches rally together, pray over their pastor and ask God to move inwardly in their shepherd's heart. In both cases, the church receives a new leader.

If you are a pastor who senses God's call to move, begin praying for a vision for the new field. However, if you are a pastor who is tired and weary, maybe you need to ask God for a fresh vision. Inevitably, in whichever position you find yourself, the question you need to ask is, "Holy Spirit, do I need a renewed passion to lead your people?"

Church leaders often go through periods of spiritual dryness or become physically and emotionally tired. The good news is the Bible promises times of refreshing from the Lord. It doesn't mean you quit serving. What it does mean is you begin to ask God to create in you a clean heart and to renew a right spirit in you (Psalm 51:10).

A pastor alone can't bring the changes necessary for a church to right the ship and begin reaching their community for Christ. It takes a changed congregation with changed leaders. That doesn't mean everyone has to be in perfect lock-step to begin moving forward. What it does mean is the pastor and congregational leaders understand their roles while protecting and providing for the success of the other.

Powerful Personal Renewal

Pastors and church leaders can find a renewed zeal to serve God – the very definition of revival. The old saying is, "If you've ever been closer to God than you are right now — you need revival!" While times of refreshing come from the Lord, it seems we hear God clearest when we place ourselves in a position to hear from Him.

If your denomination has conferences, retreats or even convention meetings, go with the intention of hearing from God. The Pastor's Conference in Southern Baptist life before our State and National Convention meetings are always inspirational. Also, State Evangelism Conferences are places where you can relax, hear a great sermon, pick up an illustration or two and find a nugget that will help you and your congregation take one more step forward. If you serve in a non-denominational church, most denominations would be glad for you to participate in their conferences. Many have no charge to attend. There are other conferences in different parts of the nation and world to help pastors and leaders hear a fresh word from the Father. Most retreats, camps or seminaries provide housing and a relaxed setting for pastors and church leaders to spend time alone with the Lord. Sometimes, merely getting out and sharing the gospel in your area or on a short-term mission trip rekindles the fire and reminds us that our fields of service are full of people who need a relationship with the Lord. At other times, down time is what a pastor or leader needs. Relax by playing golf, going fishing, taking a motorcycle ride or enjoying a favorite hobby. Pastors and leaders need to clear their heads and spend time listening to the Lord.

Powerful Principles for Leading

Some principles of leadership seem obvious. As you listen to the Lord, you need to get ready to lead biblically. The first principle of leadership is SOMEONE is going to lead. If a church goes through a leadership vacuum, someone will assume the role of leader. However, when a church has a pastor and someone other than the pastor takes the role of leader, the church suffers and moves in an unbiblical pattern. Unless there is a biblical reason for the pastor not to be the leader, everyone needs to submit to God's plan. One biblical reason for a need for someone other than the pastor to lead is if the pastor has a moral failure and the church is taking steps toward godly, church discipline. Another reason may be, God moves a pastor to a fresh field and a new flock of sheep. Then there is a need for someone to fill the leadership vacuum, but only for a short time. That may mean a group from within the church or an interim pastor from outside the church leads. There are a few reasons for this to happen but all are temporary.

Pastor, your calling is to be a servant leader under the direction of Almighty God. Church leader your calling is to fill a void and then step aside to let God's pastor lead your congregation. You should be the pastor's best asset. Be dependable. Be available. Be one who puts out the fires of discord in the church and one who fans the flames of revival. Be an encourager. The church needs a pastor and great leaders. The church also needs each of these to lead appropriately for the church to be healthy and a model of Christlikeness.

Adrian Rogers went to Bellevue Baptist Church in Memphis where the deacons were the leaders. He didn't chastise them for their strong leadership because it was a role given to them in the past. Instead, he took 45 minutes, once a month, to teach his deacons what the Bible states about their role as servant leaders who help the pastor with pastoral ministries. It only took a couple of years for the teaching to inspire the deacons' leading. Rogers peacefully, transformed a deacon-led church into a pastor-led church with a willing group of deacons who wanted to serve the Lord and be used by Him in a powerful way.

A second principle of leadership is to lead by example. Never ask your people to do something you aren't willing to do. That doesn't mean pastors or leaders are perfect by any stretch of the imagination. However, it does mean you are willing to change where God wants you to change. You are willing to go where God wants you to go. You are willing to stay where God wants you to stay. You are willing to say what God wants you to say.

Do you want your small groups to adopt a new strategy? Lead a small group to embrace and champion the new strategy. Do you want your people to be more evangelistic? Start sharing your faith several times a week and tell appropriate stories about those opportunities. Do you want your people to be generous? Teach them to be generous by your generosity. Do you want your people to be more loving, missions-minded, or great servants of others? You be more loving, missions-minded and a great servant of others.

An old football coach's phrase is, "Do the worst first." What do you like to do the least? If you are a people-person, you may struggle with studying and the alone-time it takes to preach and teach. If you are studious, you will probably struggle with spending one-on-one time getting to know your people. Whatever your weakness is, do that first because most people gravitate toward what they do well. If administration is a weakness, take care of those things first. If visiting the sick or prospects for your church is the hardest for you, schedule visits at the first of the week or the first of the day, whichever one is appropriate. Whatever you do, your people will do. As a leader, those who watch you lead will not do more than you. As a pastor, if you don't do what you are called to do, someone will do it for you and the church will suffer from it. Leaders should lead.

A third principle of leadership is to help others catch your vision and make it their own. In biblical times, a shepherd would lead his sheep from the front of the flock. His sheep would hear his voice and follow him. They knew he would care for them, provide for them and protect them. Even when the sheep went astray, he would leave the 99 safe sheep, to find the one lost sheep. There are several reasons a shepherd would do these things. One reason is he is responsible for the sheep. They are his livelihood and the owner charged him with keeping the sheep safe. A second reason is he is accountable to the owner for the sheep. The sheep are not his but they are under his watch. The master did not charge him with making the sheep what they are not, but he is to make them all they can become. Your sheep may not be "Grade A" sheep, but they are your sheep. Now help them be the best they possibly can be for the glory of the Lord.

A saying that is frequently used is, "If you are a leader, look behind you and see who is following." If no one is there, it is time to reevaluate. Why aren't the people following? Sometimes it is their fault. Sometimes it is the leader's fault.

The goal of the pastor is to move your people from where they are, to where God wants them to be. If you drive them, as the cowboys would drive a cattle herd, your pushing will only get you so far. As the old saying goes, "Don't run rough-shod over them." A roughshod horse was a horse whose shoes had the nail heads protruding from the shoe, allowing them to penetrate the ground to provide better traction on slippery surfaces. In battle, roughshod warhorses would inflict pain and destruction when stepping on the enemy. You can only inflict pain so many times before your people will turn on you. Remember, your people are not your enemy. When you have to tell people you are the leader, you are certainly not the leader.

If the people are not godly, and usurp the biblical roles God has prescribed, they are not going to allow you to lead them, no matter what you do. They are out of biblical community and fellowship. As pastor or as a church leader, you have to determine God's will about your participation in this ministry. God calls men and women to be strong and faithful to lead a congregation toward a healthy, biblical model of ministry. He even calls people to lead in part of the journey and then calls new leaders to take the people into the Promised Land. Only God and you can determine this.

A friend told of an amazing event in the ministry of a "horse whisperer." The horse a church provided for him to work with was acting very strange. Exasperated, he told one church leader there was something wrong with the horse. In just a few minutes, the horse fell over dead. After covering the horse with a blanket, he was given another horse with which to work. After using his gentle techniques, it wasn't long until he was riding the horse. During his invitation, he uncovered the dead horse and said to the crowd, "Now you can surrender your life to the Lord and be like this beautiful, working horse, or you can be like this first horse, walking around sick until you die." The story is the same with some churches. They walk around sick, causing others and themselves heartache. Unfortunately, the dysfunctional church will cause great damage for the kingdom and great destruction in the lives of newer Christians.

Another principle of good leadership is to lead with love. D.L. Moody described his method of sharing the gospel as loving people into the kingdom of God. Pastors should love their people even after they are in the kingdom of God and immersed in the life of the church. Leaders in the church should be leading people into a vibrant faith in the Lord while demonstrating love and how to be a great church member. By doing so, you will teach multiple generations how to love one another and continue a healthy work of the Lord.

When you begin to lead as a servant leader, the question becomes where does God want you to take His people. Optimally, it is on the wonderful journey of being a committed disciple of Jesus. There are two spiritual aspects of the journey. First, there is the aspect of inward spiritual disciplines. The church should see leaders faithfully pursuing inward disciplines such as prayer, Bible study, giving to the Lord's work, Scripture memorization and devotional reading. Likewise, a disciple should also possess outward disciplines that affect the life of the church. These include service in the church, service through the church, inviting someone to the church, and inviting someone to faith in Christ. While these are not all-inclusive, they do create a list to measure someone's spiritual walk.

Powerful Strategic Planning

When the pastor and church leaders start making strong disciples, God begins to trust the congregation with new people. Why is this? It is because a true disciple will always be looking for someone else to develop into a healthy disciple of Jesus. So how does a leader guide a church to be ready for the people God sends their way? Strategic planning is the way.

Wayne Jenkins, a Baptist leader in Louisiana has worked with over 1,500 churches annually for more than 25 years. He described the iconic Flake's Formula as something Arthur Flake observed not developed. Don't think a programmatic approach will automatically grow a church. However, the steps Flake outlined allows you to lead your people to be ready for what God can do through them if they become committed followers of His. The following are the five steps Flake observed:

1. **Know the Possibilities:** Do you believe Jesus when he said, "The fields are white unto harvest?" Jesus says the opportunity is present. Who is this congregation equipped to reach? Where do they live? What is it going to take to reach this target group? Will this congregation reach these people?

2. **Enlarge the Organization:** This means you have grown enough people in their spiritual walk that they might become new teachers and leaders to take care of the people coming into your congregation. God expects you to do life together as a church family. Good families do whatever it takes to provide for the needs of each other. A church family needs to provide

adequate teachers and leaders who will help those new members grow in Christ. What new classes do you need for all age groups?

3. Provide Space and Resources: It is one thing to decide you need new classes; it is another thing to determine where to put them so others can join. If God is blessing you with new people, they need a place to grow into reproducing disciples of Jesus. What books do you need to facilitate a class? How do you care for and equip their children?

4. Enlist and Train New Workers: If you develop a mindset of growing disciples who want to serve, then you are in a position for God to continue to add to His kingdom through this particular faith family. This doesn't happen automatically. You have to plan to grow people through the Word of God to become those new, mature believers who share and teach the Word of God.

5. Go after people: Do not develop a mindset of, "We've built it, now you all come to our house." Jesus tells hurting people to come to Him. However, to the church, He commands us to go to the hurting. Where are people hurting and in need of the peace, love and hope of Jesus? They are your neighbors, your friends, your acquaintances, and your family. In most communities, every third person is not on anyone's church roll. So every third person you see tomorrow at the gas pump or grocery store, is without something like a church family to care for their needs and to share life together. Don't be satisfied with a anemic formula that doesn't include an emphasis on disciples investing in the life of other disciples.

Flake's ideas are not a magic formula. However, this is a strategy for God to grow people. When you develop true disciples, it allows a church to grow deeper and wider at the same time.

Powerful Planning with Purpose

A good leader understands the basics for moving a church forward with a strategy that includes all aspects of the work God calls His church to accomplish. The first basic need is planning with purpose. The planning is not about great ideas. It is about God's ideas. Let God give you the vision, then you carry out the vision in His power. One of my favorite statements by Jenkins is, "Many churches live for 52 disconnected, consecutive Sundays." Connect the dots and move forward with purpose.

A leader offered this thought, "In our church, it seems like we just do things the same way over and over. It never occurs to us there are others who would like to participate." People are the greatest resource of the church. There is a lot a church could accomplish if it would use its greatest resource effectively. Plus, new people want to be invited into the life and work of the church. They want to feel as if they belong. Plan to use your people.

Utilizing a calendar and a list of new people helps to accomplish both the goals of effective planning and using our best resource. If a church, through whatever structure they have, will sit down with a calendar — the calendar will almost dictate a direction for most major events God wants to use in the life of the church (New Year's, Valentines Day, Easter, Spring Break, Summer Break, Return to School, Thanksgiving and Christmas). The calendar provides so many opportunities for camps, retreats, revivals, special gatherings, Vacation Bible School – the list is almost pre-made. Make sure you combine the event/need with the correct people with the giftedness to meet the need or perform the task. Don't put the proverbial square peg in a round hole. In addition, don't just sit around waiting for a burning bush to know what to do. Begin planning, implement the plan but listen to God. Just remember to plan with purpose.

Think about the Macedonian call of Paul, Silas and Timothy to take the gospel to Europe for the very first time in history. Luke joins them during this narrative in Acts 16. Watch the pronoun shift from "they" to "we" as you read (remember Luke is the writer of Acts). Those guys were not sitting around doing nothing while waiting for God to move them. They already had a God-sized, God-like, God-honoring plan. They were prepared to take the gospel to Asia Minor, but twice the Holy Spirit would not let them. As soon as God spoke, they stopped their agenda and got on God's agenda. The Bible says they immediately made plans to go into Macedonia. Plan with purpose but be ready for God to change the plan if He so desires.

The second basic need in creating a strategic plan is preparation. What are you going to have to do differently to reach your goals? Money may have to shift from one item to another. Materials and resources may have to shuffle to accomplish these goals. Training may have to occur. If everything in a church such as money, resources, rooms, and materials are sacred cows, the church can never move forward.

The third basic need in strategic planning is promotion and enlistment. These are two different aspects. Promotion is getting the announcement of the plans into worship guides, on the media screens, in the small group or Sunday School classes and maybe from the pulpit. Promotion is also about getting the information outside of the church to the people you want to reach. It may be through a media blitz on social media, television or radio. It could be newspaper ads or publicity fliers. Maybe through an organized prayer walk and door knob hangers you get the word out about your event. Enlistment is different. It is actually engaging and inviting people to get on-board. You and your team personally ask people to do certain things to carry out the plan. You need to find workers, childcare, greeters and helpers. Find people who will enlist others to do tasks to help you reach your goal. The best way to build a crowd for an event is to have a crowd working the event.

People ask how do some churches lead so many people to the Lord. Salvation is all the work of the Lord. However, the work of sharing the gospel is relegated to us. Why were 3,000 people saved and baptized on the Day of Pentecost when Peter preached? Forget the spiritual answers for a moment and think of the most practical. The answer is there were at least 3,000 lost people listening on that day. It is very simple. It is not rocket science. If you want to see God do incredible things in your church, get lost people under the hearing of the Word of God. The more lost people you go to with the gospel or the more lost people you attract to your campus, the more people you will see get saved. Once they receive Jesus' salvation, start the new believers on a journey of complete discipleship so they become healthy contributors to the work of the church.

The fourth aspect of a strategy is to produce. That means you will actually do the work God puts on your heart to accomplish. The old joke is, "If five frogs are on a log and one decides to jump off, how many frogs do you have left on the log?" The answer is five. The one just decided to jump. It didn't say he actually jumped. What does a church need to do to produce? Hold the event. Start the ministry. Do the legwork. Enlist the people. Open the doors. Do something. Sometimes it is more important to do something wrong than to do nothing. Quit talking about it and do it. Plans are merely words on paper until you place them in motion to accomplish God's purpose.

The final aspect of a strategy is to evaluate. After every task God leads you to accomplish spend time in evaluation. What worked? What didn't? What can we do better? Where did we miss the mark in God's eyes? Is this something we feel God is leading us to attempt again? These five questions and others you may discover will put you way ahead of what some churches do — of all sizes. Many are so glad the event is over, too much time elapses before a proper evaluation of all aspects of the task is completed. Remember, there is nothing wrong with an event failing. The only ministries that don't have events that fail are the ministries that are doing nothing.

The next few chapters of this book are designed to help you, as a church leader, hear from God about the functions of the church. Pastors, you need to hear from God. There are things you will learn or think about that you need to lead the sheep to work through with you. Church leaders you need to discover your giftedness and approach your pastors with ideas. The Bible calls pastors and leaders to be administrators and members to be the ministers (Ephesians 4:11-12). Each one has a role in the plan. While this work will cover things such as plans and strategy, it is more about you listening to God. The question for this chapter is: "Holy Spirit what are You saying to me about my leadership? How do you want me to equip the saints you've trusted to me for ministry?"

DISCUSSION QUESTIONS

1. If you have a pastor, pray for him to have a God-sized vision and a renewed passion to lead your church in revitalization. If you don't have a pastor, pray for leaders to realize the need to plow the fields to prepare the congregation for a new pastor. Pray that the new pastor will see the community with a fresh set of eyes and an invigorated heart to lead you to do something new for the Lord.

2. What can we do to become a church that can be led by a servant-minded pastor?

3. Are my preferences more important than process of change to reach our community for Christ?

4. If my pastor were to lead us on a new path with a servant's heart, what could I do to encourage others in the church to follow him?

5. How can we be more strategic in our planning as a church?

6. Who is someone new I need to invite to be a part of a ministry?

PRAYER

Lord,
What are you calling me to do for your kingdom's sake? Help me to be one who equips and encourages church members to accomplish the work of Christ through this church family.
In Jesus' Name.
Amen.

CHAPTER FOUR

ARE YOU PLEASED WITH OUR WORSHIP

Holy Spirit, Do I See Worship Through Your Eyes?

One of the most visible things a church does is gather for worship. It is central to the life of the church. Those outside the faith most readily identify the church with this element. People seek to find pleasure in worship by choosing a church that uses forms of music, preaching and teaching that appeal to them. Churches try to connect with their community through stylistic elements of worship. However, worship is not about our pleasure. Worship is for the One who died for us. It is to honor and bow before the King of kings and the Lord of lords. Too many times, we ask everyone but Jesus what He thinks of our worship. Our next question in this process is to ask, "Holy Spirit, will you reveal to us if the Lord is pleased with our worship of Him?"

Defining Worship

Worship in itself contains the idea of "bowing down" or "bending the knee." The picture is of a loyal subject bowing before the king to show loyalty, respect, and admiration to the ruler's authority over the subject's life. Psalm 95:6 is an expression of this: "O come, let us worship and bow down: let us kneel before the LORD our maker." Only the Lord is worthy to receive our worship, our honor and our praise. It is His demonstration of love to sinners that draws us to Him. The sacrifice of the Lamb, who gave His life as our substitute on Calvary's cross deserves worship. He who satisfies the wrath of God that rightfully should fall on us is to be praised. Understanding the cost to Jesus for the removal of our deserved eternal separation from God's Holiness, causes the overflow of worship and praise from the redeemed. We cry out because the resurrection of Jesus is the complete overcoming of death and the grave, which sets us free and guarantees that heaven is the home of all who will believe He is the Way, the Truth and the Life. His righteous rule at the right hand of the Father is the rightful place for the King of kings. He is the Lion of the tribe of Judah who waits for word from His Father to return with victory and triumph in His hand. All hail King Jesus! There is no greater cry of worship. All hail King Jesus!

You can study many aspects of worship in your evaluation and searching for the heartbeat of the Lord. Some aspects of worship are based on feelings, while others are based on facts. Is there an expectation of God moving in lives during your worship services? Are people worshiping to the point they want their lost friends and family to join them? The first question is based on feelings; the second question is based on facts — the numbers demonstrate the answer.

Common Practices of Worship

There are common practices in worship that have existed since the first-century church. A good place to start is to ask the Lord's opinion of our worship through these. Lists of the elements of worship vary, but we will ask about five.

Prayer

First, "Lord, are you pleased with our use of prayer in our worship of you?" As He answers, you may examine various aspects of prayer in worship. Is there a time for private prayer? Do different people pray during worship? Is there a real emphasis on talking to God and hearing from God during worship? Does prayer become an exciting part of worship, just as it is a somber part of worship? Does our corporate prayer bless, offer thanksgiving, seek to adore God, confess sin and address physical/spiritual needs?

Corporate prayer, much like evangelism, is a spiritual discipline that is more caught than taught. When people listen to others pray, it helps formulate in their minds how they ought to pray. Public prayer is something that a believer needs to have the opportunity to do in order to become more comfortable praying in front of others. Just as a pastor goes through the agony and nervousness of preaching for the first time, the same happens to a person who is asked to pray in a worship service. That is why small groups provide an excellent venue for new believers and intimidated believers to pray in a less overwhelming setting. True disciples learn to pray. Out loud. In front of people. So that others hear you. Why? Because part of true care and worship is the bearing of each other's burdens and bringing them to the Lord. Prayer is important in worship and in the growing life of the church.

Singing

Second, "Does our singing bring glory and honor to you alone Lord?" Martin Luther said, "Next to the Word of God, the noble art of music is the greatest treasure in the world." Whether our style is traditional anthems and hymns or our style is rocking on electric guitars, drums pounding like a second heartbeat in our chest, the One our singing must be directed toward is God. Is He pleased with our participation in the celebration of His majesty?

There are those, regardless of style, who choose to make the song service about their personal preferences or the preferences of the congregation. "Do I like this music? Is it my favorite song or style?" You should plan the music with the objective to lead the individuals God has trusted to your faith community to a place of worship directed toward Him. When singing is for individuals instead of the Eternal Lord, it becomes entertainment. "Lord, what can we do to make sure Your people are seeking You and not their top ten favorite hymns in church?"

Since worship is a verb, it must be an activity of action, not a place picked for its ambiance. Matt Redman, a contemporary worship leader said, "In the end, worship can never be a performance, something you're pretending or putting on. It's got to be an overflow of your heart."

Sometimes individuals blame their lack of planning on the Holy Spirit. I had one man tell me he never planned. He just let the Spirit guide him when he stood to lead the congregation. It was amazing that the Holy Spirit only led the man to approximately ten different songs. While his statement sounds spiritual, it is merely an immature excuse for a lack of planning. Surely, the Lord, who is omnipotent, knows enough to lead you to plan, practice and prepare in advance. I am not opposed to spontaneity or the Lord changing your direction. That should happen on occasion. But, you owe it to the Lord to allow yourself every opportunity to hear from Him. God does not have a hard time directing; it is His people who have ears but do not listen. Let God speak to you, then through you.

Quality is important. The Bible says, "Whatever you do, work at it with all your heart, as working for the Lord, not for human masters, since you know that you will receive an inheritance from the Lord as a reward. It is the Lord Christ you are serving" (Colossians 3:23-24). No matter what style of music you choose, it should be played to the best of your ability. That covers all areas of your music ministry from instruments, to vocals or to sound engineering. Practice allows you to provide the best quality of worship to the Lord that your church members are capable. You never want your sound or what you sing and play to distract worshipers from hearing from God.

Quality should be the key to all aspects of the worship service. Start on time. Have smooth transitions between the elements of worship. When someone speaks, it should be thoughtful and not rambling. The thoughtfulness should extend to announcements, a welcome to guests, prayer times and even the dismissal. You should do all things as if Jesus Himself were sitting in the congregation, because He is.

If God leads you to change the music style do it with grace and purpose. Understand music speaks to people's hearts and when they think of church, many times they think of the music they sang when they were growing up. The church has hurt itself when it relies only on hymns and songs from a bygone generation. Each generation should use its creativity to sing to the Lord. Otherwise, we stifle the gift God has put in the hearts of our contemporaries. At the same time, we should not neglect the gift of music from other generations. However, there are people today who think Jesus himself sang from an old Baptist hymnal.

When you decide to change, do it graciously. Then demonstrate clearly where and why God has led you to offer worship to Him in a new way. Change with purpose. Don't change just because you can or as some say, "To keep them on their toes." Why do you include the music you do? Educate the congregation. Maybe not every music genre will appeal to them, but show God's people that you are trying to teach the deep truths of God in the various languages of the community the church is reaching.

Giving

A third aspect to evaluate is giving. When it comes to money some churches do everything they can to downplay giving and others stop at very little to get all they can. If giving is an aspect of personal worship and it has been a part of the history of Christendom, maybe we need to ask the Lord how we can make it an exciting part of the worship of the Lord.

I was a guest preacher in one congregation that broke into applause when they had the opportunity to give as a part of the regular worship service. I have to say, I loved it. Other churches have placed boxes at the exits and never mention giving, only placing a comment in the worship guide as to where to drop off offerings. It seemed as if they were apologizing for providing members an opportunity to do what the Bible asks. Giving shouldn't be overemphasized nor should it be underemphasized. Wherever you are in the spectrum, have you ever asked God, "Lord, are you happy with the hearts of our people when they give? Are we making this aspect of worship something that brings glory to you and makes committed disciples of your followers?"

Preaching

Fourth, the preaching of the Word of God must be the focal point of our worship. When the Word of God is preached with power and the intent of the Scripture is taught and applied to daily life, then we are reflecting a biblical understanding of the preaching moment. Gathering corporately to hear the Word of God taught is a biblical mandate. The Word of God should be presented in a way that the God of Scripture is the focus, not the cute, pithy sayings of a preacher. That is not to say that good illustrations or memory devices shouldn't be used. This is far from the truth. However, good illustrations and memory devices focus the hearers on the point of the Scripture and serve to help the hearers remember the great truths of the text. These things should not seek to highlight the cleverness of the preacher.

Billy Graham said, "The test of a preacher is that his congregation goes away saying, not 'What a lovely sermon!' but 'I will do something.'" The question you may want to ask is, "Lord, is the Word being communicated in a fashion where people are hearing it and applying it to their lives?" Then you may ask, "Lord, how can I be more effective in communicating the deep truths of your Word?"

Not only does the pastor have a responsibility to feed the sheep with the Word of God, in order for worship to be that special moment with God, the people and leaders have to come with expectation. Bring a Bible. Bring a pen. Bring an open heart. Bring an intention to hear. Bring a longing for brokenness. Bring ears that will listen. Bring hands that will take action. Bring a friend with a need. Bring an encouraging word to the pastor. Bring a mind that is fixed on Jesus. Bring a contrite spirit that is prayed up before arrival. Bring peace, calm, joy, anxious longing. Bring these to God and worship like never before.

Ordinances

The fifth element is the ordinances of the Lord's Supper and Baptism. This should be a time of celebration, reflection and deep conviction. Churches sometime go to extremes on these areas of worship. They can be either so somber that they appear as a mystical ritual observed only by monks in a cave or an addendum attached to the beginning or the end of a disjointed worship service. Some churches calendar these aspects of worship with much rigidity. Many churches go so far as to place in their constitutions or bylaws when the ordinances must be observed.

You may want to ask the Lord these types of questions. "Lord, when we observe the Lord's Supper and Baptism are you pleased with how I plan it?" "Lord, how can our staff or leaders place more of an emphasis on the deep meaning of these ordinances?" "Lord, are the ordinances an extension of our worship or an addendum in your sight?" "Lord, how can we change what we are currently doing so that people see the Lord's Supper in light of your substitutionary atonement for our sins?" "Lord, how can we change what we are doing with Baptism so that the picture of death, burial, resurrection and the new birth is portrayed clearer?"

The bottom line of worship is are we making much of Christ and is our worship of Him changing our lives to conform to his image. "Holy Spirit, is our Lord pleased with our worship of Him?"

DISCUSSION QUESTIONS

1. Do you truly believe others sense a vibrant move of the Holy Spirit in our congregation? Why or why not? Be sensitive to others with this answer. A critical spirit is not helpful. However, an honest evaluation, in love, is needed.

2. Can we improve the flow of our worship service? Are we offering the best quality of worship we can with the giftedness of our people?

3. What are some ways to improve our individual worship? How can I better prepare for worship?

4. Is the Lord's Supper and Baptism meaningful in my life? Why?

5. What are some ways you have seen other churches celebrate the Ordinances? Are there ways to magnify and celebrate more vibrantly what the Lord has accomplished for us when we participate in the Ordinances as a family of faith?

PRAYER

Lord,
Our desire is to magnify and lift up your Holy name. Help us to rely on you, listen to you and bless you. Move us to a place where we surrender all areas of our lives to you in order to worship you every day. Make our ears sensitive to your Spirit and our minds open to your Word to lead others to see you in our worship.
In Jesus' Name.
Amen.

CHAPTER FIVE

ARE YOU PLEASED WITH
OUR EVANGELISM

Holy Spirit, Will You Help Us to Go and Grow?

The move is always away from evangelism, not toward it. People love doing ministries for the Lord, but very few love sharing the gospel of the Lord. Even ministers allow other things, not necessarily ungodly things, to supersede their passion for sharing the message of the Good News. There are committee meetings, visits to shut-ins, Bible studies to prepare, newsletters to write, social media to visit, family time, recreation time and worship services, not to mention denominational meetings and other gatherings. The list is huge. Ministers can do many good things and miss the best. We must not forget Paul admonished the young pastor Timothy to, "Do the work of the evangelist." What should we ask of God as we think about evangelism? "Holy Spirit, are we focused on a balanced approach of meeting the spiritual need of salvation in our community and focused on growing the faithful believers in our church?" The second question would be, "Do we need shift our focus to create a proper balance?"

Evangelism does not have to be difficult. It is merely having spiritual conversations with individuals in order to share God's plan of redemption that is available to all who will believe. A short definition of evangelism is bragging on Jesus by sharing the Good News about Christ.

The Pastor and Evangelism

Three major factors influence a church to be evangelistic according to evangelism professor, Jake Roudkovski. The first is the pastor's personal practice of evangelism. If the pastor doesn't adhere to the biblical admonition for him to "do the work of the evangelist" (2 Timothy 4:5), how can he lead others effectively to fulfill the Great Commission (Matthew 28:18-20)? The pastor is the lead under-shepherd and must model a personal commitment to sharing the gospel. The second factor is the pastor's use of appropriate stories of sharing the gospel. Obviously, the pastor should never share confidential aspects of any discussion. However, he should use stories of his opportunities as a way to encourage believers to have similar conversations with people they meet. Not only should the pastor tell of the opportunities he has to lead someone to Christ, he should also share lessons he learns when he misses or overlooks an opportunity to share the gospel. He should help people see opportunities to work in "fields that are white unto harvest." Finally, the pastor should provide training for his congregation to learn the skills necessary to share the gospel effectively. Without a plan or without some forethought, a person will stumble through sharing the gospel and may be a hindrance instead of a tool in the hands of the Holy Spirit. One key is to offer multiple ways for people to learn to share their faith. No single method will appeal to every personality in a congregation. Offering several models will help introverts and extroverts learn and embrace an active evangelistic lifestyle.

The pastor's personal practice of evangelism is vitally important. Most ministers know they should share but they don't because of an introverted nature or because they believe the latest line about what will or won't work from some guru's blog who is not a practitioner. Let me be very frank. What works is what you use. People are always looking for a new gimmick, that one thing that is going to set the woods on fire. It doesn't exist. Just begin being honest with people and loving them enough to invest and impart the gospel in their lives.

It doesn't matter if you use tracts, the Roman Road, a marked New Testament or the bridge analogy drawn on a napkin. The more you share the gospel the more you will encounter people who will place their faith and trust in Jesus. The less you share the gospel the less you will encounter people who will place their faith and trust in Jesus.

There are people with whom you are going to have to build relationships in order to share the gospel. Other people will immediately be receptive because the Holy Spirit has been using additional believers and His Word to prepare their hearts for the harvest. Scripture demonstrates both types of witnessing encounters in the life of Philip. The relationship model was shown when Philip told Nathanael about Jesus. Nathanael had questions. Philip brought him to see Jesus. Nathanael even had a question for Jesus before trusting in Him (John 1:43-50). An immediate instance of salvation occurred with Philip and the Ethiopian eunuch. The Ethiopian was reading the Scriptures and Philip being led by the Holy Spirit explained the gospel to him. The man immediately committed his life to Christ and identified with Christ through baptism (Acts 8:26-38).

Planning for Evangelism

Planning is important to a proper evangelistic focus. Your church calendar should be your friend in planning for evangelistic events, outreach opportunities and worship services. Wayne Jenkins, Evangelism Director for the Louisiana Baptist Convention, said, "Most churches operate for 52 disconnected, consecutive Sundays."

Planning a year of evangelism is not difficult. You already know you are going to have some key events you can work around: New Year's Eve, Easter, Vacation Bible School, Youth and Children's Camps, Back to School, Fall festival and Christmas. Many churches will also schedule a revival-type of service in the fall, spring or both. Realize just planning to hold an event is not evangelistic planning. You should have goals to reach adults, youth and children based on how God has trusted you the previous year. If you baptized ten people last year, evaluate what God used to lead those ten people to salvation. Capitalize on the things you discover next year. Have a goal to baptize one or two more in each age group, asking God to trust you with that number of souls again. Then pray for a movement of God, asking Him to do even more than you can think or imagine. Every event you have as a church provides you an opportunity to train a few more people in evangelism. Set a budget to accomplish the goals God gives you. Then work the plan.

Planning for Follow-up

An important aspect of evangelistic planning that is often overlooked is follow-up. Every event you have, from worship services to block parties, needs to have a way to gather information for follow-up with your guests. When you get that information, start utilizing it immediately. A phone call or an email from a staff member or church member thanking the individual or family for attending is very important. If possible, schedule a time to visit the guest. That visit may be at their home, a coffee shop or even the church office.

A common response I hear is, "People in our community don't want a visit." I'm not talking about pouncing on guests. A great door opener is to let guests know at your event that you consider them a vital part of your church ministry and you appreciate their attendance. Let the guests know you want to pray for them and that you are going to do your best to schedule a time to pray God's blessings on their family. People appreciate prayer. We should be doing this naturally.

Don't use a bait and switch approach. Go with the full intention of prayer but look for opportunities or an openness of the guest to engage in a spiritual conversation.

Genuinely get to know them and pray that God opens the door for such a conversation. Understand, you have to be intentional about sharing the gospel. It won't just happen. You need to learn how to take a conversation from golf to God. Some people will be like the Ethiopian Eunuch, ready to begin a relationship with Christ immediately. Others will need time to ask you questions and search the Scriptures. Be open and ready to walk down either road with this new friend, no matter how long it takes.

Planning for Balanced Evangelism

Find a balance in evangelism. Don't just hold events where people have to come to your church to get to know you. Go to them. Find avenues of ministry in the community. One church recently had 1,000 members and guests go to an impoverished neighborhood to paint over graffiti, clean overgrown lots and help with repairs on the homes of some of the neighbors. Through that ministry, they were able to affect the community for Christ, help with discouraging neighborhood blight and had opportunities for spiritual conversations and prayer with residents.

Smaller churches may consider partnering with an ongoing ministry or find projects more suitable to their congregation. It may be serving at a food pantry. It may be reading to students in a nearby school. It may be cutting the grass for an elderly neighbor. These are only ideas for compassion ministry evangelism. Other ideas are to hold a block party in a neighborhood where you have members live and can invite their friends.

ARE YOU PLEASE WITH OUR EVANGELISM

One rural church held a progressive fishing tournament in church members' ponds. In another church, the men in a Sunday School class went on a hog hunt and each brought a lost friend. They hunted hard, prayed hard and studied the Bible hard for two days. Several men came to faith in Christ through this ministry. A ladies group met at a local gathering place for a stamp class. One of the ladies had specialized tools to create cards and pictures with the stamps. They invited their lost friends to join them. The class began with prayer for one another and a short devotion. The ideas are limitless. What do you like to do? Do it with the intention of engaging the lost, sharing Christ and helping new believers grow in their faith.

Prayer as a Component of Evangelism

Everything in evangelism must be bathed in prayer. While many people pray, evangelistic praying is seldom heard in our church gatherings, other than a generic prayer for the lost. The 1857-1858 Layman's Prayer Revival in the United States saw one million people give their lives to the Lord. Scholars estimate that if such a movement of God occurred today ten million people would be saved in a two-year window. Men and women gathered in meetings during that period to pray for the lost. In one town, a woman turned in a slip of paper. It read, "A praying wife requests the prayers of this meeting for her unconverted husband, that he may be converted and made an humble disciple of the Lord Jesus." After the prayer request, one burly man stood up and said, "I am that man." Everyone was ecstatic. Then something else happened. As soon as he sat down another man arose. He said, "I have a praying wife and I'm sure I'm that man." Before it was over, seven men stood to their feet to say pray for me. That prayer meeting led to a revival where 500 people professed faith in Christ.

Paul expressed his anguish and concern for the lost of Israel. He was so concerned for the Israelites' salvation that he wrote he would gladly give up his own salvation if all of Israel would be saved (Romans 9:1-5). Paul would go on to say, the desire of his heart and his prayer was for Israel's salvation (Romans 10:1). Jesus himself was broken for the people of Jerusalem. He wept for them because they could not see His peace and destruction was going to overcome them (Luke 19:41-44). Jesus prayed for believers to be unified so that the lost world may know who He is and that God the Father loves them (John 20:20-23).

There are various ways prayer can be used in evangelism. To help the church go out into the community and see the needs of people, churches can organize a prayer walk. It is a simple process of walking through a neighborhood praying for what you see. If you see children's toys, pray for the family in that home to come to Christ. Pray for your opportunity to help them raise their kids in the love of the Lord. If you see a handicap ramp, you know someone has a special need. Pray for that person to be surrounded with Christians who will help them and share the love of Christ with them. You will be surprised how many conversations will begin just by walking through your community praying.

One word of caution, when asked about what you are doing, don't use the phrase, "We're praying for your neighborhood today." People will automatically think the worst. "Why are you praying over my neighborhood? There are others worse than mine." Instead, say something such as, "We are praying over our city (or community) today and I have the privilege of praying here. How can I pray for you?" If it is impossible to walk your community, you can drive. The negative aspect to this approach is you won't have the conversations that you would if you were walking. The positive is that you are seeing and praying for the needs of your neighbors.

As you seek to influence your community for Christ, ask the Holy Spirit to show you opportunities to refocus your congregation so there is a balance of reaching the lost with the ongoing process you already have to grow people in their understanding of the Bible. The opportunities are abundant. Jesus says the laborers are few. Ask God to help you find ways to lead your people to reach their neighbors, friends and family for Christ. "Holy Spirit, are you pleased with the way we reaching outward and growing inward?"

DISCUSSION QUESTIONS

1. Have I shared the gospel with someone new this week? Who has come to faith in Christ because of my personal witness lately?

2. How many ways do I know how to share my faith? When was the last time I learned a new way to share Jesus?

3. Whom have I taught to share their faith?

4. List five people to pray for who are not in a vibrant, growing relationship with Jesus? If you don't know someone who is lost, how do you think that makes Jesus feel?

5. Are we effectively following up with people who attend our events, worship, etc.? What can we do differently?

PRAYER

Lord,
Please open my eyes to those who need you this week. Help me to see the spiritual needs of the people I encounter this week in my work, travel, pleasure or daily adventures. Thank you that you have a purpose for me. Help us plan for events that will allow our people to share their faith on and off our campus. What do you want us to do? Make our hearts sensitive.
In Jesus' Name.
Amen.

CHAPTER SIX

ARE YOU PLEASED WITH OUR DISCIPLE MAKING

Holy Spirit, Are We Growing to Reflect the Image of Christ?

The art of making disciples is easy and difficult. It is elusive and captive. Most of all it is a command that we must take seriously. Making disciples is a topic of much discussion. Is making disciples a mass event or a small group event? Is making disciples a focus on a few for an extended period of time or a massive group effort? The answer is — Yes. It is all of these.

A disciple is one who is a learner/follower. A Christian disciple is one who is a learner/follower of Christ. The process of making Christ-followers varies from church to church, but the goal is to help an individual become a completely committed follower of Christ. From the start of the early church the devotion to teaching and learning the message of God became a daily task. It is still a necessary goal of a church wanting to move people forward in the

Christian life. The question we should ask the Holy Spirit is: "What do we need to change to help Your followers grow closer to the image of Christ?"

A Clear Process for New Disciples

A church needs a clear process to walk someone through when he or she becomes a follower of Christ. Some may include other steps; however, we can break this big process down to seven simple steps to help a new believer get off to a good start. First, they need to learn verses about the assurance of salvation. Doubt causes stumbling and a fluctuating reliance on the Holy Spirit. Satan is going to attack a new believer as quickly as he can. We must help these men or women stand strong in their new faith. Second, there is the need for a fervent prayer life. A new believer needs to learn to communicate with God on a personal, intimate level. Jesus taught us the Model Prayer, which contains elements of prayer a new believer needs to discover. Paul taught us to pray without ceasing. A new believer needs to realize what that means and looks like as they go throughout their day. A third step is Bible study and devotional reading. There is a need for both. Devotional reading of the Bible with a life lesson helps the new believer begin to find answers for life's situations in the Bible. Bible study helps the new believer to dig in and learn the deep truths of the Word of God.

The fourth step is Scripture memorization. Memorizing Scripture helps the new believer hide [God's] Word in their heart so they will not sin against God (Psalms 119:11). The memorized Word of God will serve as a lamp to their feet and a light to their path (Psalms 119:105). The fifth step of getting off to a good start is attendance in the local church. Through this step, the new believer learns with others who are struggling and thriving to do life together. The gathering of the church to tell God how good He is in song, prayer, preaching, communion, baptism and all the other aspects of worship needs to become a time of expectant, anticipated fellowship. It is not something you have to do. It is something you get to do — something you do with joy and excitement. The sixth step a new believer needs to take is to start sharing their faith immediately. Just as people planted the seeds of the gospel in the new believer's life, a new believer needs to seek opportunities to tell others what Jesus did for him or her. A mentor can help tremendously in this area to model witnessing and to help the new believer see opportunities that God provides every day. A final aspect of a new believer's launch into the Christian world is to understand it is up to an individual to discipline himself or herself to grow in Christ. While there are others who will help you in the community of Christ, it is ultimately up to you to make discipleship a part of your life. At the same time that it is up to you to grow in Christ, we have the model of Jesus walking alongside His disciples to be an encourager, an accountability partner and a mentor. A new believer needs to take personal responsibility for his or her growth and at the same time be willing to allow a stronger believer to walk alongside to offer support, encouragement and accountability.

When you have the process clearly defined for a new believer then this systematic process becomes a journey for those who are growing in Christ. Those who have walked with the Lord need to be encouraged in their journey to go deeper, to find more and to see what it means to be a servant to all. A disciple isn't one who merely occupies a pew. A disciple sees himself or herself as a bondservant to Jesus. When a disciple goes to work, it is with a kingdom purpose. When a disciple participates in recreation, it is with a kingdom mindset. A disciple begins to ask questions such as: "Why does God have me where I am?" "What should I be doing for the Lord in this setting?"

The disciple reflects Christian growth in the brightest manner when he or she serves through the local church. You want a believer to begin asking questions like: "How does God want me to give of myself to those who gather to worship?" "How do I help others grow to be like Christ?" "God, will you help me see areas that I can fix so an unbeliever can hear you clearly or another believer can grow closer to you?" A church should help a disciple learn how to discover, use and grow in the spiritual gifts God has given him or her to grow the Lord's church. At the same time, growing believers need mentors to speak truth to them and encourage them as they mentor someone else.

Intergenerational Focus

One danger in some of the growing churches today is the focus on a particular age group. A church that focuses on reaching young adults exclusively doesn't have seasoned adults to mentor the younger adults. The same becomes true with an older congregation that has no younger adults. The Bible clearly speaks of older women teaching younger women things such as how to love their husbands and to learn what is good. Older men are to set an example for younger men in faith, sound doctrine, patience and love. The Bible shows us that we need one another. There is a danger when a church gets out of balance.

An example of the older helping the younger became apparent in the economic downturn in 2008. In one congregation, I watched older adults talk to younger adults about the lessons they learned as children growing up during the Great Depression. The older adults prayed for the younger members and taught them the Scriptures that sustained their families during those lean, very difficult years.

I've had the same blessing happen in my life as a young man. I remember an older deacon who gave me an opportunity to speak in a nursing home. After the service, he offered great tips to connect better in that environment. He spent time with me and helped me grow in sharing God's Word because he cared. He showed me Bible verses to help me and other verses that he learned were beneficial to someone in a nursing home.

One of my childhood teachers taught her greatest lesson to me on her deathbed. I visited her in the hospital and became distraught at her impending death. She looked at me and said, "Quit worrying about me. I'm fine. If I didn't have this disease, I wouldn't have these great opportunities to share Christ with doctors and nurses I would have never met."

Younger pastors like to use the term "doing life together." That is a great phrase. However, it is merely a reconstruction of what older folks have said for years; "Our church is a family." Doing life together is what family is all about. It's about raising kids together. It's about helping each other through hard times. It's about walking people through divorces, death and daily drama. Although people outside the church do similar things, the difference is you do it in Christ. You share with one another to build each other up and to strengthen the body of Christ. In these life events, with your Bible in your hand, you study in small groups; you study in coffee shops; you mentor one another. Together. With a kingdom purpose.

Intentional Small Groups

It's that measure of intentionality that elevates great discipleship. You need a clear path. Classes that meet on Sundays or other days of the week to help a person become a growing disciple should have three basic ingredients. First, you need a teacher who is mentoring another person to teach. This will make sure the classes are self-perpetuating or giving birth to new classes as they grow. In addition, this will help keep the classes to an appropriate size to meet the needs of members effectively. Second, you need a person who reminds disciples of others who are lost or undone with the Lord. Maturing disciples are constantly looking for people who need God's salvation and those who need to renew their relationship with Him. This person also reminds the class of the process to walk new believers through when individuals come to Christ. Third, every class should have someone who reminds disciples of the opportunities to minister to people with needs inside and outside of their class. If every class would start with these basic ingredients, many of the other aspects of growth will originate from here.

Intentional Investments

As you ask God about your disciple making process, ask God if he is pleased with how you are investing personally in the lives of a few. Part of the disciple making process is to invest in future leaders. A leader should be investing in the lives of those with leadership potential. One pastor friend selects a group of men annually in whom he invests. He says, "These men know my wife and me well enough that they know where the forks and spoons are in our house." When asked what he does with the group he is apt to reply, "I just pour my life and my vision for our church into them. They are going to be our next generation of leaders. The byproduct of this investment is they are extremely loyal because they've learned they can trust me." What a great word for pastors and for the disciple making process.

Discipleship isn't just about knowledge. It's about investment. The investment is in the lives of others with clear intention of helping that person to grow to look like Christ. You know your process is working when a disciple begins to make disciples. He or she is then reproducing the process in others. The church can make that possible with a clear overarching vision, an intentional step-by-step process and an emphasis on reproducing the process in and through the lives of new believers.

In order for this process to take shape in a church, it has to be built into the culture of the church. It's not instantaneous. It's an emphasis that must pervade the heart and the life of the church. When it is working, celebrate it. Celebrate when someone leads another person to Christ. Celebrate when classes embrace this task. Provide opportunities in the worship service for the older to teach the younger. Create opportunities for the younger to express what they are experiencing — their hopes, their fears, their dreams and their struggles. When the younger members share, it helps the older folks in the congregation empathize and learn what steps are necessary to help disciple the younger. We're supposed to bear one another's burdens, to pray with one another, to study with one another — to laugh and cry as we help each other live the victorious life. Let's do life together, as a family.

Ask God to give you a vision for a discipleship process that will work in your congregation. Discipleship is more than class time. It is family time, tied to intentional learning. Ask the Holy Spirit to guide you to understand how your people are already helping one another grow in the Lord. Then ask Him to guide you to a process that is transferable to help a new believer get started strong and then for a growing believer to go deeper. "Holy Spirit, are we faithfully leading your people to become reproducing disciples who reflect the image of Jesus?"

DISCUSSION QUESTIONS

1. Do we have a clear process to help a person grow in his or her walk with the Lord that an average church member can explain?

2. How can our small groups do life together in ways that are more effective?

3. What is important to a young family that may be looking for a church home? Are we meeting those needs?

4. Do we offer a variety of times and ways a person can learn to grow in Christ? Do you think it is important to offer a variety of times and ways? Why?

5. Have you ever been closer to God than you are now? What needs to change?

PRAYER

Lord,
Guide our minds and hearts to a process that will help your new children become growing disciples. Help our goals be pure. Help our goals be intentional. Holy Spirit, convict us when we look to grow a church instead of growing people to look like you. Focus our attention on being stewards of the people you place before us. Let us see individual needs as we plan for moving our congregation forward in faith.
In Jesus' Name.
Amen.

CHAPTER SEVEN

ARE WE EXPERIENCING
TRUE FELLOWSHIP

*Holy Spirit, Are We Fully Committed
to the Life of the Church?*

Being alone in a crowd is possible in a church. Many people will enter a church but never experience true fellowship. It is entirely possible to be a regular in church, participate in many events and yet never have true fellowship. Fellowship is a multifaceted diamond that needs to have light refracted from different angles.

Definition of Fellowship

Uncovering the true meaning of fellowship begins in the root of the meaning, common. In this instance, it is tied closely to terms used for common ownership, mainly of land. The Church has one Owner and many who are responsible for her stewardship. While there are not multiple owners, every believer should have a sense of proprietary concern for her wellbeing. For our purposes, we will define fellowship as the true expression of one who is fully committed to the Life of the Church. Our question for the Lord is, "Holy Spirit, would you reveal to us how to help this church participate in and cherish the special bond of fellowship with each other through You?"

Fellowship with Christ

Life is capitalized in our definition of fellowship because it indicates the term Jesus used to describe Himself in John 10:10, "I am the way, and the truth, and the life." True Christian fellowship begins in a surrendered life to Christ. Jesus is our life and Jesus becomes our life. When we enter into a relationship with Jesus, things change. Different phrases are used in the Bible to describe the change. One term is "born again." We are birthed, brand new, through the Spirit of God. To sin and self we become dead and we become alive to God our Savior. God the Father cries out over us as the Prodigal's father cried out, "My son who was dead is now alive again." Paul describes the special salvation relationship with God as "putting on the new man." His description is like exchanging old clothes that have an overpowering, smell of sweat and the street, mixed with the putrid alcohol-vomit laced stench of the world and being transformed through a warm bath, with a freshly laundered, hand-pressed, change of clothes and just a dash of cologne. However, the meaning is deeper than merely an exterior change. It is the same kind of transformation on the inside, an exchange of the stench of death for the fragrance of new life. The Bible describes it as God calling us into fellowship with His Son (1 Corinthians 1:9).

84

Fellowship as Christ's Family

Fellowship with Christ starts on the inside of a new believer and moves to the outside. Life in Christ is personal but never private. The new believer's heart begins to resonate with other believers because Jesus is their Life too. It becomes family taking care of family — not the dysfunctional kind but as the ideal family. This type of fellowship loves one another and is willing to take hard stands to build up one another. It is not a wishy-washy fellowship that spouts anecdotal accolades; instead, it is one that holds each other accountable to restore and build character. This fellowship bears each other's burdens and prays for one another, fervently and effectively in righteousness. It is an amazing love.

Fellowship as Suffering

Fellowship can take on hardship because of the change in one's life. Not everything in the Christian life is rosy. Many things will be difficult. The Bible doesn't say that we will not go through more than we can endure. It does show that we will not go through more than God can endure. The Bible says there is fellowship in the sufferings of Christ. Paul said he rejoiced in his sufferings for the gospel. Certainly, Christ suffered faithfully to fulfill the will of the Father and likewise, we as Christians may suffer at the hands of an ungodly world.

It should be the Christian's privilege to endure the ridicule and scorn of the world. The apostle held it dear. Moreover, fellowship with Christ's sufferings brings blessings in the life of the believer. Jesus' sufferings should drive the Christian to his knees and to cry out with the loudest praise. It is through the sufferings of Christ that the believer is freed from eternal death, the righteous wage of sin. Jesus' shed blood is a covering, turning the scarlet sinner white as snow. Jesus' cruel death on an old rugged cross was a death of substitution and atonement. The sacrificial Lamb died a death we should have suffered and directed the wrath of God upon himself, instead of on those who have received Him. Atonement is an action of Jesus toward a Holy God for the sins of the whole world (1 John 2:2). In the act of suffering and resurrection, Jesus provides the way for humanity to be brought to God and have peace with God. Therefore, whoever calls upon the name of the Lord will be saved (Romans 10:13). As a matter of fact, Scripture says that as many as receive Him, to those who believe on His name, Jesus gives the right to be called the children of God (John 1:12). His sufferings and resurrection clear all the hurdles for our adoption into God's family.

The extent to which Christ has suffered for us is an example to the Church. Since Christ came to serve instead of to be served, how should the believer be toward others in the Church? Moreover, the Christian should learn how to serve a lost and dying world to reveal what a great love the Father has bestowed on us. The Bible says, "Let your light so shine before men, that they may see your good works, and glorify your Father in heaven" (Matthew 5:16). The light of our lives should reflect the grace of our Lord so the world can see the validity of what He has done in us and can do in them. Your life should make the world want to savor the goodness of our Savior.

Four Aspects of Fellowship in the Church

Fellowship will reveal itself in many aspects of the life of the church but we'll look at four. First is the aspect of prayer. There is nothing more beautiful in the life of the church as when members spend real time in prayer. How many times have you been guilty of saying, "I'll pray for you," and then walk away and forget? All of us have. However, to counteract my forgetfulness, I've tried to start praying immediately with the person about the need. Another way we can seize opportunities for deep prayer with one another is during a Bible study class, whether that is in a Sunday School type of class or a home group. A class that doesn't take the time to fervently seek the Lord on one another's behalf, is not acting in true fellowship. Church members can pray with one another during invitation times or even when walking out to the parking lot to leave. Prayer is intimate and personal. It is fellowship and following the lead of Christ.

A second aspect of fellowship can be developed while serving the needs of people in the church. A personal experience for me was during the death of my father. A group of ladies came by to help my wife while she waited for me to return from an out-of-town meeting. These wonderful, godly women finished the dishes, helped pack the bags of our two young boys and prepared a small meal before I arrived. We gathered our bags and were sent off to mourn, knowing a great church family loved us. The biggest aspect of that day was not was done for my family, but what my church family did together — time and time again. They loved one another. How many opportunities are there to serve widows, senior adults, special needs families, single mothers, divorcees, those recovering from addictions, the bereaved, the grieved, and those who are struggling to raise children. How many more needs can you see in the life of your church? Every one of those needs can bring the church closer to one another and to Christ — true fellowship.

The deep bonds of fellowship help people stay connected to a church. A question that needs asking is, "Why would someone drive by other churches to worship with our congregation?" The deep roots of fellowship is usually the answer why people do. One family came to a church through a ministry to those who struggle with addictions. They were a young family with beautiful children. The husband had an addiction problem that led to a real possibility of imprisonment. They were struggling with their marriage, finances and how they were going to survive. Through this ministry, members constantly surrounded them with prayer. People cried with them. Listened to them. Loved them. Provided for some financial needs. It wasn't long until the message of the gospel penetrated their hearts and the husband, wife and oldest daughter received Christ and were baptized on the same day. The family plugged in to the life of the church and began serving where they could while growing in their faith. There were ups and downs, but the church loved them through the hard spots. Now, years later, this family still drives an hour both ways to church, sometimes several times a week. Why would they do this when they pass hundreds of churches on their way to worship? The answer is fellowship. True fellowship.

A third aspect of fellowship is service through the church to your community. When church members engage in a common work of serving people in need, they form a strong, lasting bond. Not everyone will participate in finding ways to serve the community, but those who do will develop friendships and memories that will not be broken or easily forgotten. For churches having problems with a lack of unity, a wonderful way to refocus is to serve. Many problems in a church grow worse when the entire focus of the church's ministry is turned inward. When church members see how fortunate they are by serving those who are hurting, the members begin to see how God has blessed in immeasurable ways and that life is too short to focus on minute, internal issues.

A church in an urban area recently went to a part of town known for drugs, gang activity and violence. They went to love the community for Christ through many acts of service. Some painted over gang-related graffiti. Others cut overgrown, vacant lots. Some worked in the local school putting a fresh coat of paint and touchups to areas that needed love for the children to have a great environment to learn. Another group walked the streets picking up garbage. Through these and many other acts of service, they had numerous conversations with people about Christ. They prayed with senior adults who were broken over the massive needs in the community, asking God to curb the violence and to break through hard hearts to bring freedom and peace. More than the bonds made with the community, the bonds of fellowship melded hearts together, forging new and deeper friendships in the community of faith and making memories that will shape the participants spiritual lives for a lifetime.

The final aspect of fellowship is that service through the church is a witness to the lost world of Christ's love and restoration. When members serve in a food pantry, a clothes closet, tutoring children after-school, or by cutting the grass of a widow, the members should seek every opportunity to share the gospel through sharing of a personal testimony, a gospel tract or Bible, or a prayer with the ones being served. Those opportunities of service and witness should be celebrated and used as illustrations of God's faithfulness in small group Bible studies or the main worship time of the church. When a segment of the church goes out to serve, they become the extension of the larger community of faith.

Fellowship is infectious. People long to be accepted and want to be a part of a group making a difference. Individuals who normally wouldn't have a spiritual conversation with you, suddenly become open to the gospel because he or she may see for the first time Christians living out their faith in a way that makes a tangible difference in their lives. Even some of the hardest hearts toward Christianity know what Christians should do. Walls are broken down when the lost world observes the church being the church. People should be saved through our acts of service.

Realize that good deeds are merely good deeds that have little eternal impact if you don't look for open doors to share the gospel with those you are serving. The heresy of the social gospel was there was much social activity with little to no gospel. As a matter of fact, many times the gospel was withheld so as not to offend. While we must share the gospel with cultural sensitivity, we must never be ashamed or hesitant to share the gospel. Our first fellowship is with God. That great fellowship drives us to embrace others with the love of Christ in order for them to find fellowship with Christ and His church.

As you think about the specific aspects and biblical refractions of fellowship, ask the Lord about what He sees in the hearts of his people in the church you attend or lead. Ask Him to search your heart for attitudes or actions that hinder true fellowship. "Holy Spirit, are you pleased with the way we foster and nurture the bonds of fellowship as we do life together?"

DISCUSSION QUESTIONS

1. Does God really want us to be our brothers' keepers?

2. What are some times in your life when the church has ministered to you?

3. Who is someone you can go to and pray for and with them today?

4. What are some ways God has gifted the people of our church? How can our gifts and abilities meet the needs of our community?

5. Is there someone who knows they could call on you any time day or night for help?

6. How have you served someone lately?

PRAYER

Lord,
Help us to understand deeply what constitutes true fellowship. Move us away from the false facades of care to a place where even the lost world is amazed by the love they see radiating from this place. May you move us from the clean, neat vision of perfect families to the place of ministry. Help us to get our hands dirty in the messiness of ministry. Shine your light through us to reveal areas of need in our own hearts. Then help us to lean on one another as we find healing for our own brokenness and joy in helping others who are broken too.
In Jesus' name.
Amen.

CHAPTER EIGHT

HOW IS OUR SENDING

*Holy Spirit, Are We Faithful to Send
Our People to Serve?*

Everyone needs the reminder to live missional lives. God has given us a purpose to live in a close relationship with Him that in turn shows real love to others in the same way we love ourselves. We are to live in a community of faith that constantly seeks, sees and seizes the opportunities God provides to go. Rick Warren said, "A great commitment to the Great Commandment and the Great Commission grows a great Christian and a great church." Our goal should be to help believers "knock it out of the park."

Most church members will never search for opportunities outside of what is available through their local church. If your congregation is going to be characterized by service, members must be given many opportunities to serve domestically and abroad. When they do serve away from the walls of the church, they will come back excited and ready to serve internally with a new vigor. A popular Scripture chorus several years ago said, "If you want to be great in God's kingdom, learn to be the servant of all."

The question to ask the Holy Spirit as you seek ways to help your fellow church members is, "Holy Spirit, are you pleased with the percentage of our people who we send out to serve you?"

There are valid reasons the Holy Spirit moves people to short-term missions. The first reason is it is biblical. It was the nature of Jesus' earthly ministry. He moved about his region of the world sharing the message of repentance and the need to believe in the gospel. In fact, in Mark's Gospel, that is Jesus' first message (Mark 1:15). Paul's missionary journeys were a mixture of short-term and longer term. The three missionary journeys saw him travel among areas sharing the gospel for approximately 2 years, 3 years and 5 years respectively. Some places he stayed longer than others.

Short-term Sending

There is a move of some to say short-term missions are inappropriate at best. The problem with the arguments presented by adherents is, even though some of what they describe happens to be relevant, it is not biblical. It is extra-biblical. It is opinion. Some of their ideas are practical, such as the need to use our resources efficiently. However, even though it may cost more for a missionary group to travel and build a church or home than it would cost to hire local craftsmen, the spiritual benefit and the burden mission trips instill in those going usually results in many more resources given than if mere money is given on the frontend. Most groups return year after year to an area to share God's love, build with the kingdom in mind, share gifts and abilities, build friendships, as well as, gain a new respect for a different culture and to hear God's call on their lives. These are just a few of the benefits. In essence, short-term missions projects actually turn into a long-term commitment to a people.

A second reason to send people on mission trips is it is life-changing. Wayne Jenkins has taken groups to Brazil for over 30 years at the time of this writing. Every year multiple churches are built, prisons are visited and revivals are preached. Annually, God blesses by granting His great salvation to approximately 3,000 Brazilians. It not only changes people in Brazil, it has changed Wayne. You don't have to talk to him long to hear the passion and burden for the people of Brazil God has placed on his heart.

Buddy Newsome is a retired police officer. He developed a motorcycle ministry in his local church that has spread to over 250 churches around the United States. Every year these groups of motorcycle riders share Jesus with thousands of people at different motorcycle events. However, a few years ago, Buddy had the opportunity to go on a short-term mission trip to Moldova. He visited children in an orphanage, many of whom have been affected by sex trafficking or exploitation. To say the least, Buddy has fallen in love with the innocent children of Moldova who have no one to be their advocate. He speaks of several as his children and talks about them as a doting father would. God has given Buddy a love for a country and for a people who need

God's love and Buddy's resources. I've heard him weep as he shared how God is moving in "his children's" lives.

The Holy Spirit has spoken to many hearts and called them to a lifetime of missions, both long-term and short-term, through being obedient to go on a church mission trip. The love for missions is similar to evangelism. Many times, it is more caught than taught.

A final reason to send people on mission trips is it is contagious. When someone gets excited about missions and returns home to tell their story, God uses that message to prick the hearts of others to join the next trip or to explore ways that they may help. Some people will only go if a friend or family member goes with them. However, everyone is affected by the spirit of revival God instills in those who will go to another nation or another region in His name.

Benefits of Short-term Sending

There is a huge benefit to the church and to the spiritual growth of an individual when he or she goes on a mission trip. First, they learn it is a big world full of hurting people who are desperate for the love of God. Instead of a small, local view, it is as if they hit the enhance button on a computer map and they begin seeing the world in a much bigger fashion. Not only do they see how big the world is but also they begin to understand they can have a personal impact on a much larger area than they ever thought possible.

Matt is a youth minister who has an incredible heart for helping his students see where God is at work in their lives. For his high school seniors, he hosts a dinner for the students and their parents. The other students are invited to attend so they know they have something special to look forward to when they become seniors. Matt gives a gift to each senior that reflects how he sees God working in his or her life. One year, he gave a particular young man a beautiful map of the world. He explained he selected a map because he was afraid with the student's personality, he might miss all of the things God could do with his life if he could just see how big the world was and the great potential he had to impact the world for Christ. That's what many Christians need. They need a vision much bigger than they've ever had. A vision that is big enough to see the potential of God using their gifts, abilities and resources to influence the world for Christ.

The second lesson is that missionary work is both hard and rewarding. The call to service is work. It requires many hours of prayer, preparation and production. It doesn't happen by happenstance. It is through committed hands that pick up the plow and looks to the end of the row to make the path straight. You can't look back and wish you were home. You can't have the luxuries of home on the mission field. It is usually a fluid operation. You plan diligently but you remain flexible to meet the needs or the changing circumstances head on with excitement and not dread. After Hurricane Katrina, I remember groups calling wanting to work at our church. They would ask what we were going to be doing in six weeks when they arrived. My standard answer during that time of crisis was, "I don't know. Here is what we are doing now but I'm not exactly certain what stage of recovery we will be in when you arrive." I would tell them the key is flexibility. If you cannot function in that type of environment, without being willing to adapt, you become a hindrance and not a help.

The work is definitely tiring. However, remember as hard as you are working, the missionaries or the people in the area may have had to work twice as hard to prepare a place for you to serve. Be gracious. Be prayerful. Be ready to work.

I was on a medical/dental mission to Honduras several years ago. We held Vacation Bible Schools and had worship services in addition to the health clinic. During the afternoon, the preaching team would visit locals or help in the clinic. One day, I was assigned to help in the clinic with a dentist. Please understand the rules for medical assistance was much different back then. The dentist had pulled so many teeth that day, that he physically could not pull another tooth. He looked at me and told me to put on some scrubs. I was going to be his tooth-puller. Now, everyone may not be cut out for such a job, but I am all over any challenge. With his guidance, I pulled several teeth that day. I still have a picture of the first molar I pulled out of a poor man's mouth. I could hear him grunting as I twisted and tugged on that tooth. He didn't know English, but when the tooth popped out, he got out of the chair and said, "Thank you, doctor." I just nodded and said, "You're welcome." I didn't see that opportunity coming at all. However, I still remember it with great fondness because it stretched me so far out of my comfort zone. God used that situation to open a door to share the gospel and provide medical attention for a man in need.

Another lesson that is a great joy to watch someone learn is that God can use your gifts and abilities for His kingdom. Many people never think of a missionary being a farmer, a plumber or a carpenter. God needs accountants and businesspersons to support missionaries and provide for their needs. Veterinarians are in short supply in some parts of the world and open many doors to share the Good News of Jesus. There is no occupation or gift that God can't use to create an avenue for His message to go forth. One South Louisiana Cajun discovered that wealthy people in South America would flock to a cooking class to teach them how to make traditional gumbo, jambalaya and ettoufee (pronounced "a–TOO–fay" for you non-Cajuns). Then she could share how Jesus gave her new life and then He threw in a large portion of what Cajuns call lagniappe, which means "something extra." She explained the abundant life and the peace that passes all understanding, which was more than she ever hoped to receive from the Lord. God can use **anyone** who is available **anywhere** there is a need with **any gift** or ability surrendered to Him for the gospel to penetrate **any heart** that is willing to receive Him.

Equip the Sent to Share

Not only does God want to use your giftedness through missions, God wants to use your voice. He uses your voice to share the Good News with others who are trapped by the bad news of the world and the worse news of sin. It is one thing to be willing to share the gospel, but it is another thing to be equipped to share the gospel. There are many simple ways to share the Good News effectively. One is with a tract. Tracts have been around as long as printing has been available. Men and women realized some folks need time to read and digest the message of Christ. Tracts also provide a reasoned approach without being argumentative. One of the great benefits of a tract is in the middle of the night when God begins to work on the heart of the person without a relationship with Christ, that tract is available on their nightstand. Another reason to use tracts on a mission trip is that the tract communicates clearly in the heart language of the people to whom you are ministering. Our colloquialisms and stories many times do not communicate well or are redundant when an interpreter tries to translate the stories or phrases into the language of the listener. A tract, frankly, keeps you on track.

A second way to be equipped is with a marked New Testament. In an informal survey, a majority of pastors I interviewed use some form of the Romans' Road to share the gospel. It is easy to remember, doesn't require a lot of memorization and is found in one book of the Bible. Their presentations of the gospel follow somewhat of a similar pattern:

The Problem of Sin: Romans 3:23 *"For all have sinned and fall short of the glory of God.*

The Love of God: Romans 5:8 *"But God proves His own love for us in that while we were still sinners, Christ died for us!"*

Life or Death: Romans 6:23 *"For the wages of sin is death, but the gift of God is eternal life in Christ Jesus our Lord."*

Repentance, Belief and Confession: Romans 10:9-10: *"If you confess with your mouth, "Jesus is Lord," and believe in your heart that God raised Him from the dead, you will be saved. One believes with the heart, resulting in righteousness, and one confesses with the mouth, resulting in salvation."* And verse 13: *"For everyone who calls on the name of the Lord will be saved."*

While others added more verses from Romans or John 3:16, all were consistent in sharing these four passages of Scripture. I do believe this is a great starting point. Every gospel presentation is unique and may require knowledge of other verses but this does create a basis for believers to expand upon as they grow in Christ. Again, be careful to work with an interpreter if you can't speak the language fluently. This will allow you to communicate clearly and effectively the gospel message.

Many people have told me that they know what to share in a gospel presentation; they just don't know how to move a conversation to spiritual things. I call it "going from golf to God." Here are some suggestions. One way is to approach it directly: "Joe, we've known each other for a while, can I show you in the Bible how God has changed my life?" Another way is to ask, "Has anyone ever shown you in the Bible how to have eternal life?" Some witnesses like to use the life and death approach: "If you were to die right now, how certain are you that you would have eternal life (or some use the phrase, "go to heaven")? A follow up to this question is: "If you were standing before God right now and He asked you, 'Why should I let you in to my heaven,' what would you say?"

Long-term Effects of Short-term Sending

The most exciting aspect of the Holy Spirit sending people from one congregation to minister to an area of need around our world is the enthusiasm of the one going. The new or renewed sense of excitement about serving the Lord the short-term missionary exhibits is infectious. God will use a work in another place to open the eyes of His people for the needs within the shadow of the sending church's steeple.

A second benefit is when a person's heart is open to missions it leads to their wallet being open to missions as well. It is one thing to give to missions, it is another thing to give to a people or project you know and love. People will give more to what they see and experience in missions than what they hear and watch.

A final benefit is those who get excited about missions will enlist their friends and family to go with them on the next trip or will help others see through their experiences the need to provide resources for the work. The former mission participant will enlist others to do the work of a missionary at home. They will get others to go with them to the prisons, nursing homes and food pantries. Others will want to learn to share the gospel with the same fervor and excitement. People will see the spiritual growth, depth of Bible study and a passion for a quiet time that begins to affect the lives of mission participants. Members will want to pray with the same passion and plead with God for the souls of an unreached people group just as one who has experienced the level of lostness in a foreign land.

When we pray for God to help our people to go into the mission field, we pray the heart of God and the burden of voices of heroes in the New Testament. Our prayer is, "God are you pleased with the number of people we are sending into your ripe, abundant fields that need laborers for the massive harvest you want to bring in?"

DISCUSSION QUESTIONS

1. What do you think it means to live missional lives or to live our life as a missionary?

2. If the key to missional living or going on missions is being flexible, do you need to change? Why or why not?

3. Do you or your church actively pray for an unreached people group? If not, where could you find a group for whom to pray?

4. Is there anything that would hinder you from praying this prayer? "God, I want to go on a mission trip for you. Will you send me?" If not, pray this prayer right now.

PRAYER

Lord,
Help our hearts and minds to focus on living as a community of sent people. We ask you to call people from our household of faith to go to places they have never dreamed they would

go. Help us to change people we would otherwise never meet. While we ask you to change others, God change me. Help me to live sent.

In Jesus' Name.

Amen.

CHAPTER NINE

LEADERSHIP PART 2:
LEADING AN UNRULY CHURCH

Holy Spirit, Will You Make Me a Leader?

Many times the Lord will call a new pastor or interim pastor to lead an unruly church on the journey of revitalization. In the Old Testament, God called Zerubbabel and Sheshbazzar to lead 42,000 Jews to return from captivity in Babylon. Work began on the rebuilding of the Temple and the city but soon languished because of opposition. Then God used Haggai and Zechariah to preach to and lead the people. The work resumed and the Temple was completed. However, it was not until the time of Ezra and Nehemiah, almost 100 years after the restoration began, that God used these two men to lead the people to rebuild the city walls, while bringing about spiritual and physical change.

Leading is a daunting task when a church is unruly. Sometimes is takes the tenure of several pastors working through the issues of the people to bring about change. Other times God breaks hearts and the change occurs quickly. However, it takes both a commitment from the leadership and the people to deal with a church that has been squabbling for a lengthy time. A pastor can't do it by himself and the people rarely do it without a point person.

The question to ask the Holy Spirit is, "Will you make me into a leader that people will follow? Will you grant me wisdom, boldness and courage? Will you give me a strategic vision that will guide Your people to please you? Will you give me a heart for the cause of Christ and a burden to help Your people grow to be like You?"

Characteristics of Successful Revitalization

Trust

One characteristic of most successful revitalizations is trust. Sometimes change can be implemented quickly. Most times, someone has already been investing in the congregation and led them to a place of acceptance of change. Usually, people respond negatively to quick change. One of the issues for leaders, both pastors and lay-leaders, is failing to realize you have been thinking and working through what change looks like for quite a while. You can't expect your congregation to embrace something you haven't given them time to process. You have to show them they can trust you. They need to see you leading faithfully and lovingly.

A good leader, whether the leader is a pastor, board, or team, helps the congregation understand and see where you are leading them. Toby Frost, a pastor in Louisiana, told his congregation, "I want you to help me build a church you will not like, but one that your grandchildren will love." After helping the people to see what that would look like, in a few months the church grew from about 30 in attendance to over 200. The buildings literally had animals coming in through the ceiling at night, running around and infesting the place with fleas. Now they have made repairs and are preparing for God to continue to add to His kingdom.

High View of Scripture

Another characteristic of revitalization, especially in an unruly church, is a high view of Scripture. The authority of the Word of God should be the catalyst for any revitalization process. By praying and studying, a leader can strategically plan sermons and studies to guide a church toward health. The book of Philippians teaches about joy, humility and unity. James addresses righteous living and serving others in a faithful community of Christ followers. A leader can speak about salvation and assurance from Romans and 1 John. Churches that are unruly need to be reminded of proper Christian conduct as found in 1 Corinthians and other books. The need for love is paramount in a dysfunctional church. John's Gospel is helpful for these messages.

A warning is relevant here. The pulpit or classroom shouldn't be used as a bully pulpit. If leaders will teach through Bible books, God will bless. You will be surprised how God has you at just the right text for the need of the moment. When you teach through books, you can't be accused of preaching "at" specific people in the congregation.

I had a man come into my office to complain about the time our students ate lunch in the school we had at our church. Because of their lunch hour, he couldn't bring food and set up early for a senior adult gathering. He demanded I change the time of lunch for the entire school for his once a month meeting. I offered him several alternatives but told him, his demand to rearrange the entire school day was not going to happen. Instead of telling the other senior adults what I really said, he told them I didn't care about their meeting or them. It was amazing how I had been preaching through James for several weeks and the week after our encounter I came to James 4 about quarrels, fighting and bringing accusations against a brother. He accused me of preaching about him, but his complaint got no traction because even his friends knew I didn't pick the passage because of him, nor did I mention the specific situation. He just picked the wrong week to cause a disturbance and God's Word addressed his poor handling of the situation. That is simply the Holy Spirit's providential work of conviction of sin, call to righteousness and reminder of the judgment to come. I've seen God handle situations such as this numerous times in the churches I've served. Leaders, be faithful to the systematic teaching of the Word of God and you'll see His hand move in ways others may not. It is not only for the benefit of the congregation but it is to your benefit too.

Long-tenured Pastors

When churches are unruly and unhealthy, pastors tend to have short tenures. Because of the short tenure of the pastor, a leadership vacuum occurs and someone or some group assumes the role biblically given to the pastor. Sometimes, what the church needs is for the pastor to determine not to quit. In some churches, it a one or two people who make it their business to runoff the pastor. Usually, they are bullies the church has refused to reprimand. If the pastor feels led to stay, and if he acts graciously but firmly, he will outlast his detractors. If the church continues this path of firing or running off the pastor, the church will face extremely decline and a slow, horrible death.

Servant-Leadership

It is not impossible to revert to a biblical model of the pastor as servant-leader with deacons, boards or ministry teams as servants who follow the lead of their pastor and who work to remove pressure from the pastor. One way of helping these groups move to a biblical model instead of a worldly model is to invest in their lives. Unless they are ungodly, unprincipled people, these groups can absolutely fulfill a great need in the life of the pastor and congregation. Working with the strongest segment of committed followers of Christ, help them to see the need for change. Through studies and time, a wise pastor will shepherd this group to help him work on shaping the larger group. Ask how to best shape the group as a whole. Ask what they would like to accomplish. Listen, learn and move with this group that you are discipling to help the larger congregation learn how and why God wants to use them to shape His people. Help them see what God could do through them to change the congregation and the community to look like Christ.

An effective way to help these groups step up to a place of service is to explain why it is so important that leaders set a high standard for the congregation. Then ask them to help you identify the minimum standards that their group should model for the rest of the congregation. As a leader, if you think there are areas that may not be covered, have a conversation with one or two trustworthy, mature leaders of the group and ask them to make sure these areas are brought up. If there is an area that you realize the team overlooked, you could ask, "What about this area? What standard should we agree to uphold?" When the group sets an agreed upon standard, lead them to decide how to hold one another accountable to help each other maintain a biblical standard. Never ask your people to do more than the Bible asks of them. Also, never apologize for expecting nothing less than the Bible requires either. When the members of this group develop the model, then they have given you permission to shape them. You will never have to address them by what you think, but you can address areas of weakness with their own words of goals, desires and positions through biblical accountability.

If you cannot get your leadership behind you for the changes that are necessary, there is very little any one or any group can do to right that upside down spiritual ship. Sometimes, churches elevate people to leadership before the individuals are spiritually ready to handle the responsibility. Just because a man or woman is a strong leader in the community, does not mean he or she will be a strong, biblical leader in a church. The dynamics between a corporate boardroom and a team or board in a church are vastly different. If they are not different, there is a spiritual problem in the church. Likewise, there are problems when pastors and churches agree to unite without a full vetting of one another. There is a high level of trust on both sides that many times is assumed and not worked through as far as ideas, dreams, goals, leadership styles and other personal characteristics. While there may not be good answers to fixing either, there has to be a better process to implement for the kingdom's sake. If nothing else, the process should slow down so each party can really get to know one another. A healthy church is dependent on leaders working together to move the work of the Lord in His church forward in a way that glorifies and honors Him.

Early Victories

During a time of transition, there are leadership principles that are proven to work. There are exceptions to every rule, but for the most part, these principles work the majority of the time. The first principle is to lead your people to victories early in the process. To do so, find some actions the congregation wants to accomplish, things that move the church forward; things that the members broadly accept as necessary.

In one church, the members told the pastor they would never pave the parking lot. The members brought this to a vote in the past but the women had shot it down. The harshness of the vote made the men jaded to the point that they said they would never again bring the parking lot issue before the church. The pastor waited until a horrible thunderstorm caused issues one Sunday. One woman broke her shoe coming into the church and everyone struggled to get inside through the mud hole created in the parking area. The pastor simply went in and asked the women's Sunday school class why they didn't want a paved parking lot, especially on days like this one. He got an earful. They quickly informed him that what their husbands were saying wasn't so and they did want a paved parking lot. Furthermore, they were sick of ruining shoes and having filthy children and cars when they left church. They explained that other issues made paving the parking lot unfeasible when the idea was first brought up. The pastor dropped a hint they ought to bring paving the parking lot up at the next business meeting. They did and the color drained from the men's faces, literally. The pastor watched a couple of the men get up and slip out the back door. However, the women wanted the parking lot and after a little discussion, the church authorized a group of men to obtain bids. They had a parking lot within the next few months. The pastor didn't do a whole lot but the congregation thought he parted the Red Sea. After that event, the congregation followed their pastor into every major objective he put before them. They knew he cared about what mattered to them and handled situations in a loving way.

Set the Bar

Another principle is for leaders to set an example with their work in the church. When someone once used the term "Deacon Board," I asked, "Why are my deacons bored? Let's get them to work." If you put people in positions of leadership, work them. Too many times, churches use groups of leaders as a ruling board, dictating the work to everyone else. If God puts an idea into someone's heart, it is not so someone else can accomplish the task. If a leader brings up an idea of what the rest of the group needs to do, if it is valid, turn it around and ask that one to put the project together, enlist the people to accomplish it and then work together to accomplish the task. If you do that a few times, people won't bring up tasks they don't really want to see through. Adopt this slogan, "Don't bring us a problem; bring us a solution."

God did not call leaders in the church to become a ruling class. In the Bible, God calls leaders to serve, to work. So work. Pastors, set the example in Bible study, prayer, witnessing, visiting, and ministering. When you do, then you can expect your deacons, boards, teams and other leaders to do likewise. As pastor, set the pace for the church in generosity, love and concern for the community. If you won't do it for the Lord, who will? Likewise, leaders who have a pastor who is a servant, serve that pastor. Hold up his arms. Pray for him. Praise him before the congregation. Encourage him. Show him you mean business by telling him who you are praying with, who you are witnessing to, how you are finding avenues of ministry and how you are leading others to do so. Put out fires for him. Protect him. People who work hard for the kingdom are too tired for petty fussing. When people are doing nothing, they'll focus on the negative. The old wives' tale is accurate, "An idle mind is the devil's workshop."

Every minister and leader will have some people who are prone to be negative or oppose ideas. There is a difference between one causing problems in the church and one who is legitimately concerned. The Bible is clear how the church is to deal with the ungodly person. There is no reason for the church to allow someone consistently to be unruly. A church that does not deal with internal problems will quickly decline. The Bible clearly gives the church a path to handle discipline in Matthew 18. However, discipline is always to be redemptive and to point people to Christ. It is not to be an iron-fisted, tyrannical action. God designed it to protect the church from those who would impose their will over the congregation.

On the other hand, a person who loves the Lord is open to godly wisdom and is willing to embrace a godly vision. The way to work with someone like this is to love that person for their giftedness and appreciate that they cause you to think through the direction you want to go. Whether you are a pastor or the leader of a team who is dealing with this person, take the time to get to know them. Pray with and for them. Spend time with them. Drink coffee regularly. Enlist their help. Use them to vet your ideas. You don't need everyone to be "yes" people. You need your ideas challenged. An old saying applies to both parties, "I don't have to like what you say. I just need to like the way you are saying it."

Four Keys for Leading through Change

Many leaders ask, "How do we lead a group through changes?" The following are four keys for smooth transitions. The first key is to have a clear objective. Never change just for change's sake. Some people think they just need to shake things up to keep the organization moving. Remember an earlier adage, "No one likes change but a wet baby." Make sure you can clearly articulate where you want to go and why you want to go there. Until the others leaders can articulate the same, you haven't spent enough time preparing for the change. True change will only happen when you can lead other people to embrace the change.

Second, learn how to make the idea the group's idea. If you are not open to allowing others to give input and to shape the idea, you are not leading, you are dictating. A good leader makes an idea the idea of the group. You must have some direction and some plan to accomplish the task, but you should throw the idea in the center of the table and let everyone contribute, shape and give life to it. When that happens you get immediate buy in and you not acting unilaterally. If you want to go it alone, remember you are responsible for all the good and all the bad that comes out of the idea. If you force the idea on people without letting them embrace it, then when it fails, they will throw all the failures at your feet. Likewise, if the idea is a success the only one who will feel great about it is you. You'll appear like the proverbial rooster crowing by himself from the rooftop.

The third key to great leadership is to help your people learn to embrace failures. The church or group that has the most ideas that fail, is the one that has the most ideas succeed. This is not referring to biblical failure. You must always remain faithful to the Word of God with your message and your ethics. This is referring to trying many things to reach new people, disciple your people, create fellowship among your people and to reflect Christ to your community. A church that is alive keeps striving for excellence and moving forward in finding ways to do the work efficiently and effectively. A football team runs many plays in a game. Some move forward. Some result in going backwards. However, they keep running plays to find something that works. A church needs to find ways to take the message of the gospel to the masses. When you begin to wait for the lost to come to you, you have left your biblical mandate to be salt and light to the world.

The fourth key to transformation is perseverance. Change usually doesn't happen overnight. It is amusing to listen to people refer to a successful actor or musician as an overnight success, only then to find out how many years and hours they spent honing their craft. Barring unique circumstances, most healthy churches get that way through persistent, long-term work. The lay-leaders are stable and remain faithful to the church for years. Staff tends to remain much longer than the average two or three year tenure. A staff member who loves the congregation and is committed to their care can make more mistakes that someone who isn't perceived to be committed to the church or community. A good word for young pastors is, if you aren't willing to stay with your people and see the changes through, don't be the one to instigate it and leave. You'll hinder the next pastor's ability to lead. Another way of putting it is, "Don't knock out the rungs of the ladder as you climb up. You or someone else may need it later."

Whether your congregation is starting over with a fresh, new pastor or if your starting over with a refreshed pastor, the key is to lead faithfully. Lead with love. Lead as a servant. Lead the church to go the extra mile by walking an extra one for them first. Each person who has a leadership role in the church must do his or her part to move the church to a place of health. Your church needs this. Your community needs this. God's kingdom needs churches to resolve inward issues to take the gospel to a world that is hurting and in pain. Take the peace of Jesus to the world. Become so desperate that you are completely dependent on the Lord. "Holy Spirit, are you pleased with the way we are leading? Will you make each of us leaders with the gifts and abilities you've given to us?"

DISCUSSION QUESTIONS

1. Is the congregation you lead considered a.) healthy, b.) needing minimal change, c.) needing a major overhaul or d.) unruly?

2. In your role as a leader of this congregation, are you committed to being a long-tenured leader or are you looking for a way out of your job?

3. Are you willing to submit to biblical, servant-leadership from your pastor? Is the church willing to do the same?

4. How can you begin to serve other people in the congregation? How can you influence others to serve?

PRAYER

Lord,
Help us to embrace serving others as you have demonstrated
service to all. May we become selfless servants. May we become
people who put out the fires of adversity in our congregation

instead of ones who fan the flames of gossip, strife, hardship, backbiting, and destruction in the House of the Living God. Correct us. Reprove us. Remind us of sin. Remind us of righteousness. Remind us of the judgment to come.

In Jesus' Name.

Amen.

Afterword

Tools and Resources @ KeithManuel.com

As you already know, you didn't find every answer for your congregation in this work. Hopefully, it did help you to ask good questions. If you take the next step of applying some answers and working to develop a strategy to get back on track, you will do what many churches never do.

Visit my website: KeithManuel.com to find a **FREE Priorities Analysis** to dig deeper into ways to examine and enhance your current ministries. It is located with The Desperate Church under the tab, Books, in a downloadable PDF.

Also on KeithManuel.com, you can explore resources for evangelism and disciple-making that I've used personally. They are linked to the company or author who created them. Some have a minimal cost. Others are free. I will update and try my best to keep all the links and resources current.

I would love to hear an update about the progress of your congregation based on your work with The Desperate Church.

There is a contact section on KeithManuel.com or you can email direct at Keith@KeithManuel.com.

Finally, check the website for additional books that are coming soon.

God bless you as you lead your congregation forward under the power and work of the Holy Spirit.

Keith Manuel

Simple, One Year Strategy

Many pastors envision a church that is an evangelistic, disciple making church. However, few understand what it takes to create that culture in a congregation. In order to change people's mindset, you must have a strategy that encourages, equips, and elevates the need for this type of environment. Your people can only catch what is thrown to them. Enthusiastically, do this ANNUALLY.

1. Training
   Hold a minimum of 2 training events annually:
   One in Evangelism
   One in Disciple Making

2. Set Goals
   *Baptize 1 more child, youth, and adult than last year
   *Start one new Sunday School Class or Small Group
   *Disciple at least one new person

3. Reach New People with a Quarterly Event
   Christmas, Easter, Vacation Bible School, ????

4. Plan to share the Gospel with one person each week.

5. Have a list of lost people you pray for daily.
   a. Pray for these 6 days a week
   b. Pray corporately when you gather with your group or class. Evangelistic praying is powerful.

40 Evangelistic Outreach Ideas

1. Evangelistic Block Party
2. Super Bowl Party
3. Homeless Shelter Outreach
4. Nursing Home Outreach
5. World's Largest Sundae
6. Gathering After a School Sports Event
7. $1 Car Wash
   (Give those who come $1 and a Gospel Tract. When they ask "Why" answer, "Because of God's free gift.")
8. Buy a Christmas Gift for a Someone You Don't Know in the Mall/Store. Include a Card Telling about Jesus' Free Gift of Eternal Life.
9. Mass Bible Distribution at Parade/Community Event
10. Door-to-door Survey
11. English as a Second Language
12. Adult Reading Education
13. After School Tutoring
14. Revival
15. Celebration of the Family
16. Parenting Seminar
17. Wildgame Supper
18. Luncheon for Community Leaders
19. Host a local Sports Team for lunch after church
    a. Recognize them in service
    b. Have a committed student share a testimony
20. Host an Outdoor Extravaganza
21. Host a Hunter's Education class

22. Host a Women's Craft class/gathering (Stamp class, Scrapbooking)
23. Hold a Back Yard Bible Club at Apartments, Trailer Park or Neighborhood
24. Host a Sports Clinic
25. Vacation Bible School
26. Community Movie Night (Town Square, Ball Field, Park)
27. Community Easter Egg Hunt
28. Host an event for Special Needs Families
29. Home renovation/makeover clinic
30. Children's Fishing Rodeo: Use ponds or safe bank for fishing
31. Volunteer to Read at a School
32. Adopt a school (service projects)
33. Prayer Walk
34. Buy the person's meal in the drive-thru behind you, leave a card inviting to church
35. Go through a neighborhood and ask for prayer needs; Pray with them; Go back to check on the need.
36. Host a Job Fair/Job Skills Training/Resume Creating Seminar
37. Host a Tea for Ladies and/or Girls
38. Host a Concert
39. Bring in an Evangelistic Team (Strength Team, Sports Ministry, X-treme sports, etc.)
40. Create a sports league or weekend sports event (Upward, Bowling, Community Basketball, Church league Softball, 3-on-3 basketball tournament, etc.)

TIPS FOR FOLLOWING UP WITH PROSPECTS

1. Make a card on each prospect

2. Get information
    a. Names of all people in their family
    b. Address
    c. Phone Numbers
    d. Email
    e. Did you come with a church member?
    f. Do you regularly attend a local church?
    g. Would you be interested in a new group to study the Bible?

3. Use prayer as an opportunity to follow up:
    Thank you for coming to our event. Even if you are a member of another church, we feel like you are a part of our church family for today. Because of that, we are going to do our best in the next few weeks to get to each home and pray God's blessings over your family.

4. Have a place on back of the prospect card to track your follow up:
    a. Email and/or letter
    b. Phone call
    c. Personal visit
    d. Provided info about our church

e. Provided devotional information about how to know Christ and grow in Him
f. Spiritual information
g. Invitation to a Bible study class

Why is follow up important?

People want to know you care. Amazingly, statistics have shown that the best first contact is not the pastor. New people want to connect with peers. Also, they expect a pastor to want to talk to them. However, the response to a church member who takes the time to get to know them and connects with them is overwhelmingly favorable. Once the connection is made with a peer, it opens the door for a pastor to have spiritual conversations too. It takes approximately seven contacts to develop a strong relationship with a guest. Don't neglect the opportunity that is provided to make a new friend, see a person come to faith in Christ, or connect with a new family of faith.

About the Author

Keith Manuel is an emerging author for church ministries, families, and children. His numerous articles appear in church related publications.

He edited *One on One: Evangelism Made Simple* and created the website WhatIValueMost.com (Read his story there). He edited three devotional guides for Louisiana Baptists. Keith has served as a pastor, professor, photographer, and denominational consultant (Sorry. No "P" for that one!).

Hundreds of churches use Keith to speak and consult in areas of evangelism, revitalization, and encouragement. Visit his website at KeithManuel.com for booking information.

Keith is a graduate of William Carey University (B.A.) and New Orleans Baptist Theological Seminary (M.Div.; Th.M.; & Ph.D.). He is married to Wendy. They have three children Keith, Jr., Jeremy, and Hannah.

Coming Fall of 2016

Packed with proven power principles for sales
and even more powerful truths to expand
your prayer life.

Notes

Notes